Marty's Musings

Marty's Musings

TALES of the GREAT DEPRESSION, WORLD WAR II, the KOREAN WAR, and NEW JERSEY

MARTIN D. JESSEN

Outskirts Press, Inc.
Denver, Colorado

Marty's Musings
Tales of the Great Depression, World War II, the Korean War, and New Jersey
All Rights Reserved.
Copyright © 2011 Nancy E. Jessen
v3.0

Edited by: Nancy E. Jessen

Outskirts Press, Inc.
http://www.outskirtspress.com

ISBN: 978-1-4327-7870-5
ISBN: 978-1-4327-7960-3

Library of Congress Control Number: 2011913302

Outskirts Press and the "OP" logo are trademarks belonging to Outskirts Press, Inc.

PRINTED IN THE UNITED STATES OF AMERICA

My father once told me, "Make sure you marry someone who will put up with you." I did.

Dedicated to my wife, Barbara Jane, with all my love.

Learning is fun! Learning is stimulating, learning is profitable, and learning makes life a lot more interesting. When I see a tree, I see a colorful sugar maple. The beautiful pink and white flower is a bleeding heart. The singing red bird is a cardinal. The maroon and white rock is green pond conglomerate. A boat sailing by is a yawl!

You enjoy things more when you know what they are, where they came from, how they work, and how they were made. Many people go through life and don't have a clue about how the wonderful world around them works. They don't understand free market systems, can't calculate a percent, or give you the correct change without the register calculating it for them. Most people can tell you the player's names of their favorite sports team or musical group, but they don't know the name of the Speaker of the House of Representatives, who is one of the most powerful people in the world.

You should look at every job, even awful jobs, as an opportunity to learn something. I have always kept my eyes and ears open, had an inquiring mind, and looked at the bright side of things. I've had a wonderful and interesting life.

—Martin D. Jessen,
4 July 2011

Contents

Chapter 3: World War II

Chapter 4: Post War

Chapter 5: Korean War

Chapter 6: New Jersey

Chapter 7: Church Stories

Chapter 8: Strictly Business

Chapter 9: Family Life

Foreword

James J. Florio
*49th Governor of New Jersey (1990-1994) & Lieutenant
Commander United States Naval Reserve (Retired)*

Marty Jessen is a good man. He is my neighbor, or more appropriately, I am his neighbor, since he has lived in our community of Metuchen, New Jersey, much longer than I have. He is a philanthropist and businessman, involved in all manner of activities in his church and the community at large.

My wife Lucinda and I have been the beneficiaries of his agricultural prowess by receiving vegetables from his extensive gardening activities. He is also a nice man.

However, it was not until I read *Marty's Musings: Tales of the Great Depression, World War II, the Korean War, and New Jersey* that I realized Marty is a deep and thoughtful observer of the human condition…someone with an observant eye for detail, with perceptive insights into everyday actions and events that are at the same time commonsensical and profound.

The startling parallels between his life experiences and mine qualify me to comment—and verify—his observations. Overriding all is a commitment to education and knowledge as a key to opportunity, and a meaningful life in general. Marty's stories illustrate time and again, that you can't fix a problem if you don't understand the problem. He brings an engineer's perspective to his lifelong quest for knowledge.

It is clear that service in the military was for him, as it was for me, a major life-shaping force. We both enlisted in the United States Navy at seventeen years of age—he near the end of World War II and I near the end of the Korean War. After active duty, we both were part of the Naval Reserve—he at Naval Facilities in Perth Amboy and myself at the Lakehurst Naval Air Station. We both financed our education in part through the G.I. Bill of Rights, and we both were granted commissions as ensigns in the United States Navy.

Marty's insights into the virtues and follies of military life are delightful! The benefits of systemic military structure he describes can be life-shaping, as I believe they were for both of us. On the other hand, the military bureaucratic foolishness that some of his tales highlight can be humorous or tragic, depending on the circumstances. His recounting of the ability to "cumshaw," the unofficial acquiring of needed materials (i.e., scavenging), brought back pleasant memories of my Navy days.

Marty's ability in his stories to glean philosophic gems out of otherwise normal life experience is stunning. Both of our experiences as very young newspaper delivery boys (he in Metuchen; I in Brooklyn for the *Brooklyn Daily Eagle*) illustrate the virtues of responsibility and basic business principles inculcated into young minds. Likewise, our common responsibility for "taking out" the ashes from our coal-burning facilities—in my case our home's entire heating system—early on pointed one to an appreciation of being part of a family network. The family network ultimately expands to the entire community or communities of interest (e.g., church, business, or political), to which one has responsibilities.

Marty brings a historical perspective that is seen in the

sequence of his tales to which I, and I suspect many of his readers, can relate. References to iceboxes, home delivery of milk and bread (I remember Dugan's Bread), and simpler times in business practices all highlight how things change. His tales also illustrate how some fundamental things have remained the same.

Marty's stories about his business career, which has unquestionably been successful, offer us a picture as to how traits we all purport to hold in high esteem are still valued. Common sense, plain direct speaking, honest bargaining—all flow as virtues embedded in the pages of this book. In an age of business speculations and clever sharpsters, this book should be required reading.

Finally, our love of our town, Metuchen, is a point of commonality that is reflected in this volume. My major contribution to our community is my wife Lucinda, whose multifaceted efforts on behalf of the town, most notably at the YMCA, are known by most. It is clear that Marty is "Mr. Metuchen" for many. He has been appropriately so honored many times over the years.

This book represents his views and values which reflect our hope that Metuchen, New Jersey, and America, even while experiencing the inevitable changes that the future holds for us, remain committed to the fundamental principles that Marty has shared with us in this delightful read...

Preface

In 2009, I began self publishing various short stories titled "Marty's Musings" in a local weekly advertising paper called the *Criterion*, in Metuchen, New Jersey. I have been telling stories my entire life. I enjoy making people laugh.

I have received a tremendous positive response from the community regarding my stories. People I don't know walk up to me on the street and tell me how much they enjoy my stories. They always mention a particular one that moves them. Now I can't go to a social function without people asking me, "When are you going to put the stories into a book?"

Well here it is—*Marty's Musings: Tales of the Great Depression, World War II, the Korean War, and New Jersey*. This collection of short stories has been organized into chapters of the varied experiences I have had or tales that others have told me. I have tried to write the stories to the best of my recollection and to be historically accurate.

The most defining time of my life was the period I spent in the United States Naval Reserve as an enlisted man and officer. I have always told "Navy" stories because I received a tremendous education—courtesy of the United States Government—during World War II, the Korean War, and, thanks to the G.I. Bill of Rights, Rutgers University. I am thankful because the lessons I learned through those varied experiences helped me be successful throughout my life.

Life is full of challenges. Hopefully the reader will gain some wisdom by examining the actions of the characters in this book, and maybe a bit of history will rub off too! I know lessons can be learned from my experiences and my mistakes.

I think it is important to sit together with your family at the dinner table and engage in conversation. My family and friends have heard me tell these stories numerous times. I am honored to share them with you.

to Jersey City on the Pennsylvania Railroad tracks. There was also passenger traffic to Perth Amboy with a station on Lake Avenue in Metuchen.

The Lehigh Valley Railroad wanted its own route to Jersey City, so it began acquiring land for the line starting at Bound Brook. It arranged to buy land in Raritan Township (Edison today) from a Mr. Marconeer—a sharp businessman. One of the details for the land sale was a lifetime railroad pass for him from his home in Raritan Township to Jersey City.

For many years afterward, the "Black Diamond Express" stopped by his house, the conductor put down a portable step, and Mr. Marconeer went to Jersey City and took the ferry to New York City.

The Edison Valley Playhouse on Oak Tree Road, Edison, was formerly the Marconeer Reformed Church. You can still see the beautiful stained glass windows today.

Another Mr. Marconeer story was when the water company wanted to purchase land on top of a hill he owned to construct a large water tank. It is good to have water tanks on high ground to get better control of the water pressure. Part of the deal was to have a fire hydrant installed in front of his house. As the water tank was built, a shiny new red fire hydrant appeared. Years after his death, it was found that the fire hydrant was not hooked up to any water lines! The devil is always in the details.

Grandfather's First Job

First an explanation. Before the invention of incandescent light bulbs by Thomas Edison in the 1870's, electric lights were arc lights. This is a light source made by placing two carbon rods close enough for the electric current to arc across. On board Navy ships, this is used for twenty-four- and thirty-six-inch searchlights. Also, in the theater, the "spot" light is usually an arc light.

My maternal grandfather, Daniel Hughes, who was born in 1868 in Dowlais, Wales, got his first job in a factory grinding square ends on round carbon rods so they would fit into a carbon lamp holder.

You may ask, "Why not make a holder to fit the round ends?" The answer is that Wales is part of England and the English just don't do it that way.

Grandfather was about ten years old and worked with several others boys that same age. They were paid by the number of rods they squared—piecework. This was done by holding the rod against the *top* of a large spinning grinding stone, one at a time.

The second day, grandfather started taking a rod in each hand and grinding each one on each *side* of the grindstone, two at a time. His production more than doubled, as grinding on the flat side was easier than on the rounded face.

Soon the other boys started using this new method. Pay shot up. My grandfather was a hero with his fellow workers.

Next, the boss noticed the increase in production and reduced the piece rate by more than half. My grandfather went from hero to villain and had to find another job.

A Land of Plenty

At the age of eighteen, my maternal grandfather, Daniel Hughes, immigrated to this country from Wales aboard a White Star Line steamship equipped with sails, the SS *Britannic*, which departed from Liverpool, Queensland, and arrived in New York Harbor on 26 June 1886. He processed through Castle Garden—America's first immigration station—which had once served as a circular sandstone fort (construction began in 1808) located at the southern tip of Manhattan Island, New York City.

A ferry took him to New Jersey to board the train to Johnstown in Western Pennsylvania. He traveled with two other Welshmen who spoke little English. Grandfather bought bread and cheese before boarding the train. His Welsh friends did not buy any food because they thought the American states, like Wales, were small, and Pennsylvania was right next to New Jersey. They soon learned how big America really is, and Grandfather shared his food with them.

Grandfather's mother had wanted Daniel to be a Presbyterian minister. Grandfather had not been sent to work in the coal mines; instead he remained in school and was well read and spoke Welsh and English.

In Johnstown, the three Welshmen got jobs with the Cambria Iron Company. The two Welsh friends got jobs as mill-hands. Daniel had worked in a steel mill in Wales and read books on the process of making steel. Recognizing his intelligence, the Cambria Iron Works started him out as an open-hearth furnace melter's helper. Under the direction of a melter, the helper places raw materials into the furnace, regulates the temperature, pours test molds to see if additives are needed, taps the furnace, and performs repairs.

The Welshmen found lodging at a boarding house, where they were served breakfast and supper. A lunch was packed for them by the housekeeper to eat at work.

After three days at work, his companions asked in Welsh how much they were being paid and what did the boarding house cost. Grandfather answered their questions and explained that the boarding house cost one-third of their pay.

Then they asked, "Are we paying anything extra?"

Grandfather answered, "No, but why do you ask?"

"We are being fed meat three times a day, every day. In Wales we were lucky to get meat twice a week. America is surely a land of plenty."

The Johnstown Flood

Twenty-one-year-old Welsh immigrant Daniel Hughes (my maternal grandfather) was not alarmed as he waded in water over his ankles to his job as a foundry laborer (a melter's helper) at the Cambria Iron Works. The date was Friday, 31 May 1889. It had been an extremely wet spring, and it was not unusual for Johnstown, Pennsylvania—built on a flood plain—to flood.

Beginning ten years earlier, the South Fork Dam—situated in the mountains above Johnstown—had been repaired and rebuilt to create a private lake for wealthy Pittsburgh steel and coal financiers and industrialists. There were concerns that this earthen dam would break, but few of the people in power took these concerns seriously.

Daniel arrived at the Cambria Iron Works at seven o'clock in the morning to start his fourteen-hour shift. There had been a torrential downpour the night before and the two rivers—the Little Conemaugh from the east and the Stony Creek from the south—that converged at Johnstown were continuing to swell their banks. The company decided to shut down the iron work's furnaces and send the workers home.

Early that afternoon, the yellow-brown water was over Daniel's knees as he waded back to the boarding house at 63 Union Street near The Point (the point where the Little Conemaugh and the Stony Creek rivers merge). The waters had risen so rapidly that the first floor of the house would soon flood. The housekeeper, Miss Jennie Anderson, asked Daniel and another boarder, mill-hand David A. Williams, to move the rugs and furniture up to the second floor.

Around ten minutes after three o'clock in the afternoon the South Fork Dam broke. The Conemaugh Lake water started its fourteen-mile path of destruction down the Little Conemaugh at a speed of forty miles per hour towards Johnstown. For Daniel, who was moving furniture, the first sign of trouble was when he heard a tremendous loud rumbling sound—like thunder. A high wall of water and debris roared down the steep valley demolishing nearly everything in its path—including downtown Johnstown. The wall of water headed toward Daniel's boarding house near The Point.

Daniel and the others scrambled to the attic and began to climb through a trap door onto the roof as the wood-frame house was hit by a wave of floodwater and debris. As the river of floodwater made its way past the house, it struck the side of the steep hill behind the nearby Stony Creek.

After hitting the hill, the floodwater and its victims flowed in one of three main directions.

The main mass of floodwater and debris bounced off the mountainside and continued downstream, where it piled up against the arches of the old Stone Bridge—a Pennsylvania Railroad bridge downstream of The Point—that had held.

Some of the floodwater backwashed off the mountainside and sent a huge wave upstream on Stony Creek. This wave destroyed the densely populated Kernville section of Johnstown.

The middle section of floodwater formed a wave that headed *back* to downtown Johnstown—destroying many houses that had survived the initial fierce attack.

This backwash wave lifted Daniel's boarding house off of its foundation and carried it *upstream* toward downtown Johnstown. The frightened passengers clung to the swirling roof of the disintegrating house.

The mountain of debris that was accumulating at the old Stone Bridge formed a nearly watertight "dam" and the waters of Lake Conemaugh temporarily reformed upon the flood plain where Johnstown had once stood. Daniel's roof-and-attic "raft" floated on the "lake" and started to *very slowly* approach the side of Green Hill near Frankstown Road. When the roof drifted alongside the very steep hill, Daniel and his fellow survivors jumped to safety.

John J. and Hannah Jenkins Davis were at their house at 131 Frankstown Road at the time of the flood. John J. Davis, a stone mason, and his sons were at the side of Green Hill using ropes and poles to pull people out of the water. The Davis daughters escorted survivors—many wounded and in shock—to their house where Hannah Davis was making hot soup. A few blankets, hot soup, fresh drinking water from a spring, and shelter for some, were provided. Over one hundred homeless people were at or near the Davis house that night.

From the porch on the Davis family's "house on the hill" was a panoramic view of the devastated valley below—where Johnstown lay in ruins. The houses and debris piled up at the old Stone Bridge started burning—as hundreds of people trapped within scrambled to get out. Throughout the night, survivors on the hill watched in horror knowing that the brightly burning mountain of flames was consuming more victims at the old Stone Bridge.

Although approximately eighty people who had survived the flood perished in the fire, the old Stone Bridge—which had been overbuilt to withstand the pounding force of the drivers on steam locomotives—had probably saved lives by preventing those trapped at the bridge and those drifting on roofs on the temporary "lake," from being swept further downstream in the Conemaugh River.

The next morning, approximately three thousand survivors were stranded along the muddy Frankstown Road on Green Hill. Cold, wet, hungry, many with injuries, they looked down into a valley of destruction—muddy water, gunk, broken boards, damaged and displaced structures, toppled railroad cars, and drowned or crushed men, women, and children.

The Davis family sons descended the hill to help rescue those trapped in the debris. They made their way to the old Stone Bridge—where crushed buildings, boxcars, barbed wire, telegraph poles, trees, and other wreckage formed a tangled burning mountain with people still trapped inside.

Surprisingly some houses were intact—either in part or in full. One of the Davis family sons, John, went into a house at the bridge and saw a kerosene lamp with a hobnail cranberry glass shade, fringed with crystal prisms, hanging undamaged from the dining room ceiling. The fire was about to consume the house so he took the lamp down and brought it back to the house on the hill.

The flood destroyed nearly all of Johnstown—records show that 396 children aged ten years or younger had been killed. A Davis family daughter, Elizabeth (Lizzie), was a Conemaugh Borough Public School teacher who had the gruesome task of identifying students at the emergency morgues.

Over 2,200 people perished that day—making the Johnstown Flood the worst man-made disaster in 19th Century America.

Just as the flood hit, Robert Pitcairn, head of the Pittsburgh Division of the Pennsylvania Railroad, was in his private railcar inspecting the railroad tracks four miles west of Johnstown (downstream of the old Stone Bridge). The train was stopped on the tracks bordering the Conemaugh River because the signal line to Johnstown was down.

Pitcairn first noticed unusual debris floating in the muddy river—small pieces of broken wood. Then people desperately trying to swim, and others clinging to telegraph poles or parts of buildings, were carried past by the swift moving current. The river became littered with debris, dead horses, cows, and humans. The train passengers tried to rescue those they could reach. Pitcairn, a member of the exclusive South Fork Fishing and Hunting Club—that owned the South Fork Dam—was familiar with the geography and quickly surmised what had caused the horrifying sight.

Pitcairn telegraphed news of the disaster and ordered the train back to Pittsburgh. In Pittsburgh, the Pennsylvania Railroad loaded trains with volunteers, laborers, and boxcars full of lumber, food, clothing, and supplies. The first relief train reached Johnstown on Sunday morning, followed by many more—but the need was staggering—with approximately 27,000 homeless flood victims.

Five days after the flood, Clara Barton, then sixty-seven, and fifty doctors and nurses of the newly organized American Red Cross arrived on the Baltimore and Ohio Railroad. They set up tent hospitals to care for the wounded; distributed blankets and food; and provided temporary housing for the homeless. Clara Barton remained in Johnstown for five months—it was the first major disaster relief effort for the American Red Cross.

The rainy evening after the flood, homeless Daniel Hughes made his way up Green Hill and slept on the cellar door under an elevated porch at the Davis family's hillside home off Frankstown Road.

The morning after the flood, the Davis family daughters were distributing breakfast to the survivors. Elizabeth, then twenty-six, brought Daniel breakfast and struck up a conversation with the handsome young Welshman. She caught his eye, and Daniel and Elizabeth were married six months later on Thanksgiving Day, 28 November 1889.

I spent most of my childhood living at my maternal grand-parents' house in Metuchen, New Jersey. The beautiful lamp with the hobnail cranberry glass shade, salvaged from the doomed house at the old Stone Bridge, hung over the dining room table—a reminder.

I would often help grandfather with his beehives and vegetable garden. He told me the story of The Great Flood of 1889 many times. I can still hear him proudly say, "I survived the Johnstown Flood and I didn't get my feet wet!"

Grandfather

In 1886, at the age of eighteen, my maternal grandfather, Daniel Hughes, immigrated to this country from Wales. He worked in the steel industry, survived the Johnstown Flood, and was superintendent of the C. Pardee Steel Works in Perth Amboy, New Jersey.

In 1922, he retired. Daniel took the trolley to Metuchen, a small borough twenty-nine miles southwest of New York City. He bought the house at 343 Main Street without ever going inside—because the seller would take his World War I bonds as payment and it had a large chicken coop with a big backyard. He wanted to raise bees and needed the coop for storage.

When my grandmother, Elizabeth Davis Hughes, saw the inside of the house she was very upset. The kitchen had a very rusty cast iron sink with a pitcher pump that pumped out of a cistern. Built in 1856, the worst problem was that the center of the wooden house had settled several inches. Most of the inside doors had been cut off at the tops and bottoms just so they could close. Needless to say, a new kitchen sink with city water was installed and the center of the house was reinforced and leveled up.

The large backyard was plowed up with a horse and a walk-behind plow. Flowers and vegetables were planted.

The beehives came "knocked down" and my grandfather had to put them together. He then installed ten wooden frames with sheets of bee's wax. The bees came by mail in a screen-sided box. Inside was a smaller box with the queen bee inside with eight or ten worker bees. This was so she would have the same smell as the rest of the bees. The bees were put in a hive, and the sugar plug that blocked the hole in the queen's box was opened. The bees ate the sugar and the queen came out and went to work. The honey the bees made helped support us during the Great Depression.

As I grew up, I helped grandfather. I liked to talk to him. I listened to many stories, some multiple times. Looking back, I should have talked and listened more. In later years, hundreds of times I wished I had asked this or that. I had a valuable resource and I was too immature to use it to the fullest.

My advice to the young folks is—talk to your parents and grandparents. Write down or record their stories. They can tell you a lot that is not in books or on the Internet. Do not be like me, looking back and wishing I had done more listening.

CHAPTER 2

Great Depression

Axel's Market

In the 1930's, before the invention of supermarkets, there were grocery stores. In Metuchen on the corner of High Street and Main Street was the National Store. The northwest corner of the Forum Theater had the American Stores Company. The corner of Main Street and Hillside Avenue had the A&P (The Great Atlantic & Pacific Tea Company). Cohen's Butcher Shop was located on Main Street opposite Highland Avenue. Finally, there was Axel's Market. It was located on Main Street (where Wernik Place is today) in a twenty-foot by thirty-foot section of a two-story house that was later torn down by the State of New Jersey.

Axel sold groceries and meat. As a boy I liked to watch Axel working by his butcher block, a three-foot-square table with a two-foot-thick sycamore top with the end grain up. He would take up his long knife, sharpen it with a rat-tail file (a thin round tapered file shaped like the tail of a rat), and then slice three pork chops. Then with a few well-aimed whacks with a meat cleaver, he severed the bone. He finished them off, wrapped them in heavy paper, and weighed it. Axel and his store were unique in town because he gave credit. Many Metuchen residents shopped there because of the credit he offered.

During the Great Depression I remember my mother, Hannah Hughes Jessen, and father, Martin Jessen, sitting at the kitchen table. On top of the table was a small pile of checks. Two were from my mother's substitute teaching jobs in Metuchen and Raritan Township. Some months the checks were small amounts—if the regular public school teachers did not get sick too often.

Then there were my father's checks. He was a machinist at Booth Machine in Lakewood, New Jersey. There were usually three or four weekly checks in the pile. Usually the discussion I would hear was how many checks (if any) were good this week.

Then the bills would be figured. Rent, utilities, sometimes a load of coal, and then what we owed Axel. When my father's checks were good and could be cashed, Axel was a very happy man. I grew up constantly hoping that the machine shop checks were good and that some schoolteachers were sick.

Kindergarten

I started kindergarten at the Washington School in Metuchen, New Jersey. Today it is called the Mildred B. Moss Elementary School. A fellow student, Adele, lived near me, and she showed me the way to walk to school. She also helped me with shoes (right and left, tying, or buckling) and generally looked after me. I have always been the kind of guy that needs help, and I always appreciate the people who help me.

We only had school for half a day. Our teacher, Mrs. Brewster, read us stories. We even got half a pint of milk and then nap time. We each had a cubby to keep our crayons and papers in. There was an open space in the back of my cubby that always bothered me. One day my red crayon rolled into that space and disappeared. Teddy, whose cubby was next to mine, decided to share his red crayon, so he broke his and gave me half. The big deal with crayons was to keep coloring within the lines.

The most interesting thing to me was a very large chest that was full of large blocks. It took two hands just to pick up one block. We built great structures with these blocks.

Then we sat down as the teacher played the piano for us as we sang songs. *Twinkle, Twinkle, Little Star* was a class favorite.

There was one song that I did not like:

Rock-a-bye baby, on the treetop,
When the wind blows, the cradle will rock,
When the bough breaks, the cradle will fall,
Down will come baby, cradle and all.

Looking back, this was pretty grim for a five year old. I always wondered why they would put a baby in a tree. Even at five years of age I knew that was not a very good idea.

Grandfather's House

When I was in first grade, my parents could no longer afford the rent on the small house they rented that stood behind a large house on Amboy Avenue in Metuchen, New Jersey. My mother, Hannah Hughes Jessen, my father, Martin Jessen, and I moved back in with my maternal grandparents, who lived around the corner at 343 Main Street.

I loved my grandfather Daniel Hughes' house. It had a big yard with a garden. My friends and I built regular huts, underground huts, and tree huts all over the property. We would walk the one block to downtown Metuchen and get orange and lettuce crates for free. We would knock the crates apart and use the wood for siding on our huts.

When I was in second grade, I got scarlet fever. I was quarantined in the house for several weeks. My grandmother, Elizabeth Davis Hughes, sat down to read with me and realized I did not know how to read at all! She had been an old-fashioned school teacher in Johnstown, Pennsylvania, and got out her old reading books. There was one book for each grade from first to sixth. She started with the first grade book. She explained to me how to sound out the words. I would read out loud to her and whenever I would come to a word I did not know, she would say, "Sound it out." It was like magic! All of a sudden I could read! Within two weeks, I was reading the sixth grade book.

I really enjoyed the books. Each one contained several stories, all of which had a moral to them. They had positive messages: work hard, be honest, do right, use wisdom, and help your fellow man.

A Young Boy's Christmas

When I was a young boy Christmas was quite an event. An early bed time for me started all the final preparations.

The fire was allowed to burn out in the fireplace. My stocking was tacked up to the mantle. A hot cup of coffee was set out with some cookies for Santa. I asked if we should put out some hay for the reindeer. I was told that they had already eaten. Then I was whisked off to bed, for Santa had a lot of work to do.

The fresh cut Christmas tree came out of its hiding place in the garage. It was set into a cast iron stand that had lights around it. My father, Martin Jessen, bought the stand at a Perth Amboy, New Jersey, church for five dollars, and our family has used this stand for over eighty years.

The lights had to be strung on the tree. The light bulbs were strung in series, which meant that if one bulb burned out the whole string was out. To fix the lights, you started by replacing the first bulb in the string, and if the lights did not come on, you moved the first bulb to the second spot. You would work your way down the line until eventually the string of lights lit up; you had just found the burned out bulb!

Then the electric train had to be set up. It was a standard gauge American Flyer passenger set. It circled around the Christmas tree. The presents were spread out around the tree. The stocking was filled starting out with an orange in the toe. Santa had worked very hard.

I dreamed that night of the electric train running around the Christmas tree. I think I heard some test runs in my sleep!

The next morning I got up early and raced down the stairway. My stocking was full, Santa's coffee cup was empty, and all the cookies were gone. Wow! As I looked at all the presents under the tree, most were unwrapped. As the Great Depression got worse, there were fewer and fewer toys and more practical gifts like clothes. Boys don't think too much about clothes, but for me I had clothes on my mind every time I saw my cousin, Erhard Oksen.

My cousin was bigger than me and when he grew out of his clothes they would be passed down to me. Whenever my cousin got some new clothes, I would look at them and wonder how long it would take him to grow out of them and how long it would take me to grow into them.

In later years I wanted a set of switches for my standard gauge train set. They were very expensive and I knew we could not afford them. Unknown to me, my father found this out. If you can't buy them, then make them was his attitude.

Imagine my surprise when on Christmas morning my train set had two switches installed. The regular Lionel switches in those days were manual. My father made electric controls—you just pushed a button by the transformer and the switch was thrown!

The best Christmas present was a hammer. I was always building things and I really appreciated my own hammer. My dad carved my initials in the wooden handle. That hammer is special to me and I still have it today.

My family was poor during the Great Depression but so was almost everyone else. I was not aware that I was poor. I had a good time growing up.

The Delaware and Raritan Canal

When I was just starting elementary school in the 1930's, our family's main form of entertainment was going for an automobile ride on a Saturday or Sunday afternoon. For fifty cents worth of gasoline, the whole family had fun. Mom and Pop in the front seat, Grandma and Grandpa and me in the back seat. The ride always ended with some Hershey's ice cream at fifteen cents a pint.

One afternoon while exploring the beautiful New Jersey countryside we were driving alongside the Delaware and Raritan Canal when we passed a steam-powered canal boat called a "Lighter." My dad sped up the car and said, "There is a lock just ahead." I did not know what a canal lock was, and all I wondered was why we would want to see a padlock.

The car pulled up alongside the canal lock, where everyone piled out, and my canal education began. My dad explained that the canal boat had come from the west in Bordentown, New Jersey, and was traveling east to New Brunswick, New Jersey, where the canal's last lock connected to the Raritan River. The canal boat would travel down the Raritan River to Raritan Bay and then possibly on to New York Harbor. He explained that canals were navigable waterways used for the transportation of goods. Completed in 1834, the Delaware and Raritan Canal system initially transported mostly coal from the Pennsylvania coal fields—this was important because Central New Jersey and the New York City area were running out of trees to burn for heating and power!

The lock we were standing by was going to lower the boat so that it could continue traveling east. Dad pointed out the closed miter gates downstream, and the raised drop gate up-stream. With both gates closed, the lock had been filled with water. While the steamship waited upstream, the upper drop gate was lowered.

The steamship glided into the lock slowly. The lock ten-der shouted, "Careful of my lock." A deckhand threw a bow line and a stern line to the lock tender, and he looped them around the bollards—short vertical posts. The lock tender raised the upper gate, and then we followed him to the huge miter gates that acted like giant doors. He opened the wickets to let the water in the lock drain down, thereby lowering the canal boat.

The lock tender called to me, "Hey young feller! Come over here and help me open the gate." I ran over to the lock. Each miter gate had a long balance beam sticking out over a curved walkway. It had wooden cleats on the walkway. At five years of age, the twelve-inch-square beam was over my head. I reached up to help, and I just barely touched the beam. "Now push!" ordered the lock tender. I pushed alongside the man, and the huge timber began to move. We opened up the gate! The deckhand opened up the other one.

We all heard the whoosh of steam as the engineer opened up the throttle. The steamship glided out of the lock. The Captain waved at me and shouted, "Good job young feller!" That made my day.

Most of the Delaware and Raritan Canal system remains intact today, and is used for recreation and to bring some of our drinking water from the Delaware River to New Brunswick. But to me, two thoughtful men made a young boy very happy. "Good job young feller!" Whenever you can, always take time to encourage the young!

The Kitchen Stove

W hen I grew up in the 1930's, we had a coal stove in the kitchen. One of my chores was to bring buckets of coal up from the basement coal bin and to take out the ashes. On very cold days, the kitchen was the only warm room in the house. In my bedroom one night the water in my frog bowl froze!

The fire box was about twelve inches wide by twenty-four inches deep. It was covered by two circular cast iron lids. There was a lifter to remove the lids to add coal, and at certain times when cooking, the cast iron frying pan or cooking pot would be placed directly over the fire.

A black eight-inch stove pipe rose from the back of the stove and angled across the ceiling into a chimney. In the vertical piece of the pipe was a damper; a circular piece of iron inside the pipe that controlled the draft to the chimney.

At nighttime, the fire was "banked" by adding coal, closing the damper, and closing sliding covers just over the ash pit. This reduced the amount of air and slowed the burning of the coal. If all the adjustments were done correctly, we would awaken to a nice hot red fire. If not, it could be a cold morning, trying to get the cold stove working again.

The right side of the stove had four gas burners. These were only used in the summertime as gas was more expensive, and besides, the coal stove heated the whole kitchen.

At the back of the stove there was a large cast iron pot with a heavy lid. This pot was for soup. The soup was usually made once a week with a soup bone. During the week various left-overs were added to the pot so that the taste changed, but it was always hot and good.

At lunchtime, my maternal grandmother, Elizabeth Davis Hughes, would make buckwheat pancakes in the big frying pan. In those days we went home from school at lunchtime. Some of my friends would join me for the buckwheat pancakes covered with Log Cabin syrup. Log Cabin syrup came in a can shaped like a cabin with the chimney as the pouring point. The pancakes were served stacked three high. Many of us ate two stacks, they were so good.

The only scary thing in the kitchen was when the long john underwear had frozen on the clothes line and had to be de-frosted and dried in the kitchen. The frozen long johns would stand up in the corner of the kitchen and as the kitchen stove did its heating magic, they would wilt and slide to the floor! The kitchen stove was a very special item in our home.

The Bootleggers

Eddie Leis was a new police officer in Metuchen, New Jersey, in the early 1930's. His father was in charge of a section of the Reading Railroad in the Metuchen area. He was getting complaints about smelly garbage on the southern banks of the railroad west of Grove Avenue.

Investigation proved it to be mash from the illegal production of whiskey. These were the days of prohibition when the Federal Government had passed a law making it illegal to drink alcohol. Some people got around the law by manufacturing their own to consume or sell and called it "moonshine." Eddie pushed the Chief of Police to investigate. Eventually suspicions focused on a house on East Chestnut Avenue bordering on Woodwild Park.

A raiding party of police was assembled. They drove up to the house and surrounded it. No one answered their knocks so they broke in. The house seemed empty, but they thought they heard a noise in the cellar.

The police rushed down into the cellar. No one was there but an alcohol producing still was cooking along. They noticed a set of shelves against the wall were slightly askew. They tore the shelves away, revealing a passage leading away from the building.

Guns drawn, they started down the narrow passage and the three front police officers tumbled into a hole. Flashlights revealed a dry cistern, half full of bags of sugar. But where were the still operators?

Further investigation revealed another tunnel leading back towards the railroad. The police charged down the dark tunnel, flashlights bobbing. The tunnel ended in the woods. No sign of the bootleggers.

The last man through the tunnel had tripped over a large stone. He went back and found the stone. It was a milestone from the Middlesex-Essex Turnpike. Today this milestone is displayed in front of the Borough Hall on Middlesex Avenue.

Further investigation revealed that the house had been rented by people unknown. The rent had been paid in cash to a teller in the National Bank. He knew nothing.

Choo Choo Trains

In the early 1930's, there were three very active steam-powered railroads traveling through Metuchen, New Jersey. The Reading and Lehigh Valley Railroads carried mostly coal from Pennsylvania to the docks at Perth Amboy and Port Reading (Woodbridge). At the docks the coal was unloaded into barges and shipped to coal-fired electric power plants and industries. The Pennsylvania Railroad transported mostly passengers and freight.

The steam engines that powered the trains burned coal to make high pressure steam that drove the engine. The exhaust steam from the cylinders was blasted up the smoke stack. This increased the draft in the fire box and made the distinctive choo choo sound.

The increased draft carried cinders and soot up the smoke stack, creating the beautiful smoke plume. Unfortunately, this plume eventually descended onto the surrounding area.

Porches and leaky window sills would receive a daily dusting. This was before the word pollution was invented. Most people thought black smoke meant jobs.

At nighttime, the Pennsylvania Railroad ran long freight trains to avoid interfering with daytime passenger traffic, just as is done today. Sometimes these freight trains would stop in Metuchen as they waited for the signal for the tracks up ahead to clear. When it came time to start up again, the engineer sprinkled sand via pipes in front of the drive wheels to increase the traction. A slow choo choo sound was made as the engine took the strain.

However, if the drivers slipped, the choo choo sound quickened. The engineer knew he had the power, but not the traction to move the freight train ahead. What was the engineer to do?

One solution was for the engineer to back the train up. There was an inch or two of slack between the couplers that connected the cars together, and by backing up he would bunch up this space. What you would hear was a loud bang, bang, bang, bang, down the length of the train. Then the engine started forward, and the bang, bang, bang, bang was heard again.

If you think about it, only one freight car at a time was starting, and the moving inertia of the moving cars added to the traction.

As a young boy living three houses from the train tracks, I would often listen to this drama. Sometimes it would take more than one try to get the train moving, which would result in even more loud bang, bang, bang, bangs. When I finally heard the steady choo choo sound from the engine, I knew that the train was moving away. I smiled and drifted off to sleep in the now quiet of the night.

The Army Flies the Mail

For a short time during 1934, the Federal Government got mad at the airlines and took away their contracts to deliver airmail and turned the job over to the United States Army. Airplanes navigating during the daylight hours used the magnetic compass. Most towns, trying to help out the pilots, painted the names of the towns on the roofs of large buildings. The easiest navigation method was to follow the "iron compass," which meant follow the railroad tracks.

Flying at nighttime was much more difficult. Some parts of the country had aircraft beacons. There used to be one in Metuchen on top of Beacon Hill, hence the name. It was a tall steel tower with a revolving search light. The next beacon was located outside of New Brunswick where U.S. Route 1 and U.S. Route 130 intersect. The altitude of the airplane was determined with an aneroid barometer, which had to be set by the local barometric pressure at ground level.

One evening in 1934, my father took me out to Hadley Field in Piscataway, New Jersey, to see the mail plane take off. The airport consisted of a large grass covered field with three hangers.

A single biplane (two wings on each side) sat outside one of the hangers. Two mechanics were fueling it up. A Ford Model A mail truck pulled up with the daily airmail. Several bags of mail were put in the forward cockpit.

Then the pilot came out, dressed in heavy flying clothes. It would be cold in an open cockpit. He had a leather helmet, goggles, and a long white scarf wrapped around his neck. The scarf was very important as it not only kept him warm; it also was used to clean his goggles when oil splattered back from the engine. The pilot climbed into the rear cockpit. The mechanic grabbed the wooden propeller and called, "Switch off." The pilot turned off the ignition switch and called back, "Switch off." The mechanic was now safe to give the propeller a few warm-up turns by hand.

"Switch on," called the mechanic. "Switch on," replied the

pilot as he turned the ignition switch back on. Then the pilot yelled, "Contact," and the mechanic gave a strong downward pull on the propeller as the engine roared to life.

The plane sat there as the engine warmed up. After about a minute or two, the engine sound smoothed out. The pilot gunned the engine; he waved to us, took a look at the windsock, and taxied out onto the grass field. He faced the plane into the wind to get the most lift, then we heard the engine roar, the plane began to accelerate; the tail lifted off, then the whole plane. It soon climbed higher and higher and turned toward the setting sun.

Today that old airfield is a shopping mall on Hadley Road. It is amazing how things change over time.

Flyers

During the early 1930's, there was no supermarket in Metuchen, New Jersey. There were separate grocery stores: bakeries, butcher shops, and green grocers. Some of the grocery stores were chain stores: American Stores Company, A&P (The Great Atlantic & Pacific Tea Company), and the National Store.

The grocery stores had wall shelves stacked with goods with a counter in front. The customer asked the grocer, who stood behind the counter, for the items wanted. He would take the items off the shelf and place them on the counter. Some stores gave credit, which let them compete with the slightly lower priced chain stores.

One of the methods of advertising was flyers. Usually once a week they were distributed by local boys. The flyers were folded up and slid into an old-fashioned wooden clothespin. It made a compact missile easy to throw twenty to thirty feet onto porches.

One summer afternoon a group of us found a bundle of flyers—over two hundred. We hauled them up to the Main Street bridge over the Lehigh Valley Railroad. There were two tracks and a nice open space. We started making paper airplanes and seeing whose plane would fly the furthest.

Soon a police car pulled up, the officer got out and leaned against the railing. "What are you doing?" he asked. We explained our aeronautical experiments. He waited as we used up the pile of paper. When we had finished, the tracks, the water-filled ditch, and the side slopes were speckled with white paper airplanes.

The police officer growled, "OK you kids, get down there and clean up that mess. Look out for trains. I'll watch."

The Icebox

During the early 1930's, refrigerators were just coming into use, while most people used the icebox. The iceboxes were varied but usually were made from wood with a galvanized steel box inside. Typically, they were about four feet high by two feet wide by two and a half feet deep. There was an upper compartment for the ice, and a lower one for the contents.

The ice was delivered by the iceman. At first, delivery was by horse and wagon, later it was made by truck. If you were a customer of the iceman, you had a diamond shaped sign that hung in your front window. At the corners were the numbers five, ten, fifteen, and twenty, representing how much money in cents you wanted to spend on ice that day. You would spin the numbers around until the price you wanted was in the uppermost corner.

The iceman, on seeing your sign, would split off the correct size piece with an ice pick, grab it with ice tongs, carry it to the back door, enter your home, and place the ice inside your icebox. Home security was not a problem back then. On hot summer days, kids would follow the ice wagon to get a piece of ice to suck on.

In Metuchen, New Jersey, on the south end of Pearl Street, Costas Ice Cream Company owned an ice plant. Large blocks of ice were made by freezing water under the floor of a room inside. When frozen, the blocks were lifted out and stored in another room, which served as an icehouse on the south side.

Sometimes I was sent to the icehouse to get a ten-cent piece. I took my wagon, walked down to Pearl Street, and paid my ten cents. The attendant took my dime, went inside, and soon a small steel door popped open and my block of ice slid out. Pickup was much cheaper than delivery of ice, so we could get a bigger piece with me and my wagon on the job.

At some icehouses, men going to work would leave their wagons parked outside and pick up ice on their way home. My Uncle Gus did this many times. Everyone's wagon was painted differently because they looked alike. One day when my father was a boy he went to the icehouse and painted Uncle Gus's wagon a different color. Uncle Gus had to wait for all the other men to take their wagon home before he could find his wagon!

The ice melted in the icebox and the water was collected underneath in a drip pan. This pan had to be emptied each day unless you owned a dog, who would drink the water.

Some of the ice came from ponds and lakes, but that is a story for another day. Refrigerators have now replaced the icebox in the kitchen, and the iceman no longer cometh.

AM Radio

The first radio I remember as a boy in the 1930's was a box, ten inches by ten inches by twenty inches long, with four tuning knobs. On top of it was the speaker; a two-foot-high apparatus that looked like the end of a French horn. It had an outside aerial antenna. This consisted of a wire leading from the house to the garage, with insulators on each end. The insulators were made from the necks of broken Coca-Cola bottles. A lead from this ran inside to the radio. This radio would only work intermittently.

A year later, my maternal grandfather, Daniel Hughes, who liked music, bought a new radio, which stood on the floor. This radio had a built-in eighteen-inch speaker. The "guts" of the radio had over a dozen vacuum tubes. These were glass tubes that were four to five inches high and had a multi-prong base. Each type of tube had an individual prong pattern so the right tube went in the right place.

If the radio stopped working you would check the tubes. If one did not heat up then you replaced it. Most of the time they all heated up, so you would remove all of them and go to the radio store and have them tested. Grandfather saved the old tubes because some of them came back to life after a suitable rest.

At that time there were only AM (amplitude modulation) radio stations. Their signals bounced all over the world, particularly at night. The big deal was to tune in on KDKA in Pittsburgh, Pennsylvania, one of the early more powerful stations.

Radio station WOR had a one-thousand-watt transmitter in Carteret, New Jersey, and, if I remember correctly, their studio was in the Bamberger's store in Newark, New Jersey. Today alongside the New Jersey Turnpike in North Jersey, you can see the tall antenna towers in the large swamps. This water filled flat area (the ground plain) provides better transmission of the AM signal.

Some of us kids had crystal sets. This consisted of a special crystal the size of a pea that we tickled with a small wire called a whisker. This would be linked to earphones and you could barely hear the radio.

There was a story of a citizen of Carteret who slept in a brass bed. If he touched the brass, he could hear WOR and could tell you what was playing. It turned out that he worked at the carborundum plant, and one of their products was grinding wheels made from carborundum. Carborundum is a compound of silicon and carbon used as an abrasive. He had silver fillings and dust from the plant in his teeth. His head had become a crystal set!

Don't Let the Ghosts Get You

Years ago, each cemetery had a caretaker, who usually lived on the edge of the cemetery. They took care of all the maintenance for the cemetery. In those days, the caretaker did all the grave digging by hand.

One hot August day, Mr. Rabinski, the caretaker, was digging a grave. He carefully set the sod off to one side and started to dig with a pick and shovel, piling up the dirt on the side of the grave. Being so hot tends to make one thirsty so he had a pint of whiskey with him. As he dug deeper and deeper, trying to reach his goal of a depth of six feet deep, he carefully gauged the drink to last till the bottom was reached. There was no air conditioning, and the coolest place in Metuchen, New Jersey, was at the bottom of the grave. After a hard day's work, he dozed off in the bottom of the cool grave.

That evening we kids were playing the last game of tag in the graveyard. We knew that we had to be out of the graveyard before dark, when the ghosts rose up. I was "it" and was chasing Willie. He jumped over a pile of dirt and tumbled into the grave, landing on top of Mr. Rabinski. With a loud grunt, Mr. Rabinski sat up and started moaning. Willie flew out of the hole running the fastest I ever saw him run and he did not stop until he reached home.

I watched Mr. Rabinski as he buried the whiskey bottle in the bottom of the grave and said, "May it rest in peace."

The Soda Business

During the Great Depression of the 1930's, a six-ounce bottle of Coca-Cola cost five cents, while a twelve-ounce bottle of Pepsi-Cola cost five cents too. Pepsi-Cola also had a quantity discount of six bottles for twenty-five cents.

We kids decided to go into the soda business. We took our wagon and toured vacant lots until we found enough deposit bottles to get our start. Small bottles had a two-cent deposit, while quart bottles had a five-cent deposit. To get started in business we needed thirty-five cents; twenty-five cents for six Pepsi-Cola's and twelve cents for the deposits.

One hot July day found us on Main Street, Metuchen, New Jersey, selling soda. We soon sold five bottles, and told our customers that they had to drink it right away, so we could have the empty bottle to return for the deposit. Then temptation got the best of us and we drank up our profit, but we kept our starting capital of thirty-seven cents.

We quit the soda business after a few days and drank up our capital. There was a jingle on the radio we used to sing:

Pepsi-Cola hits the spot
Twelve full ounces that's a lot
Twice as much for a nickel too
Pepsi-Cola is the drink for you*

*PEPSI-COLA is a registered trademark of PepsiCo, Inc.

Uniforms

During the 1930's, the Metuchen, New Jersey, YMCA (Young Men's Christian Association) had a church basketball league. Our church took part with a team of nine boys. In those days most people were too poor to afford sport uniforms. So our solution was for one team to take off their shirts, becoming the "skins" team, and the others to keep their shirts on, and they became the "shirts" team.

Our team came up with an idea for uniforms. Each player brought a white undershirt. We then bought some blue dye, and we dyed all the shirts. Three of us put our pants in the dye too.

The next Saturday we were on the court with our blue uniforms, and we won! We were so happy going into the locker room, but then we took off our shirts and we found ourselves dyed blue. A hot shower and soap did not remove the blue dye from our skin. Three of us were blue from top to bottom and it took several weeks before it wore off. The games went back to the "shirts" versus the "skins."

The Bees Are Coming

During the Great Depression, we had twenty or more bee-hives behind our house at 343 Main Street, Metuchen, New Jersey. The sale of honey helped supplement the family income.

In the springtime, the stronger hives raised a new queen bee. The old queen and the new queen fought and the loser left the hive with many worker bees loaded with supplies. This was a swarm. They flew up in the air and usually headed to a tree where they hung in a bunch about one half bushel basket in size. Scouts were sent out to find a new location: a tree hollow or the wall of a building.

My maternal grandfather, Daniel Hughes, would spot the swarm. A new empty hive, with preformed wax comb bases, would be set up with a board ramp leading to the entrance.

Usually the young queens flew higher and landed higher above the ground than the older queens. For the high swarms, a peach basket on a long pole was used. The bees were shaken into the basket and then dumped on the ramp in front of the new hive. The bees were buzzing all this time. Suddenly, the tone of the buzz changed. The queen had entered, and all the bees pointed toward the hive and marched up the ramp to their new home, ready to go to work. Busy as a bee!

One springtime, a woman from Maple Avenue called and said, "There is a swarm of bees in my backyard. Could you take them away?" The reply was, "Maybe."

Grandfather prepared a hive and asked me to go with him.

I was about ten. He took his bee veil, gloves, and a basket. We met the woman and she showed us the swarm. The bees were on a low hanging branch. Grandfather asked if he could cut off the branch. "Yes," she said, "Just get those bees out of my yard."

Grandfather put on his veil and gloves, cut the branch, put it over his shoulder, and we started walking home. As we started up Main Street, grandfather asked me to go ahead and warn the people.

Picture a young boy going up through the downtown Metuchen business district shouting, "The bees are coming! The bees are coming!" Behind me, grandfather walked with most of the bees on the branch and many others buzzing about his head.

I was amazed at my power to clear the sidewalk. People ducked into stores or crossed to the other side of the street. When we reached the new hive, the swarm went in with no trouble. Grandfather explained that this was probably a wild swarm. It was too far away to be one of ours.

All it takes to give power to a ten year old is a swarm of bees!

Tin Foil

When I was a boy, most men liked to smoke pipes, cigars, or—the most popular choice—cigarettes. In the 1930's, very few women smoked. A package of cigarettes had an inner wrapping of paper covered with tin foil. One of our methods as boys to get penny candy money was to collect the tin foil and roll it up into a ball. When the ball of tin foil was the size of a softball, we would sell it to the junk man who traveled the street in a beat-up truck, ringing a bell.

Many smokers threw their empty cigarette packs away, littering the roads and sidewalks. Traffic lights were always a happy hunting ground. If too many kids were in the tin foil business, the pickings could get pretty slim. Then we would head out to clean up the highway—U.S. Route 1.

After us future entrepreneurs had gathered up half a bushel of empty cigarette packs, it was now time to strip off the tin foil. This required good fingernails and lots of patience. This was an excellent time for conversation, usually a discussion of the penny candy market. Our softball size tin foil ball would be sold to the junkman for fifty cents.

He knew we had to divide the money up, so he would pay us in nickels. For two of us that would mean twenty-five cents each.

We had learned the lesson that patience increases the enjoyment, so we agreed to limit ourselves to five cents a day spent at the candy store. At the candy store, we had some major decisions to make. There were licorice sticks, bubble gum with a baseball card, all day suckers, lollipops, and other tempting morsels, all for a penny each.

The all day sucker and the bubble gum had the advantage of lasting the longest, and the baseball card was an added bonus. Baseball cards could be gambled for at school, with the game being to place your card on a spot three feet off the ground and then let go. The next player would do the same thing. As the cards fluttered down they would cover a large area. The winner would be the first player whose card touched another player's card, and he would win all the cards on the ground. Sometimes there would be ten or twelve cards on the ground before there was a winner.

I often thought how wise we would have been to save the cards instead of wearing them out with our play. Oh well, such is life without twenty-twenty foresight.

Learn to Swim Week

During the Great Depression the Metuchen, New Jersey, YMCA (Young Men's Christian Association) had an annual "Learn to Swim" week. I was ten years old when I signed up. As I arrived at the "Y" with my towel, I was joined by twenty-four other skinny boys. We went down to the locker room, undressed, and then into the shower room. Most of us were in tremendous need of a good cleaning. We took our cold shower, and then walked up the ramp to the pool. The door was closed as we all waited.

After what seemed like an eternity, the door flew open, and as we filed past the instructor, he patted each of us on the head to make sure we all had taken a cold shower. We marched down to the shallow end of the pool and stood around the edges.

The assistant instructor jumped into the pool, grabbed the side, and demonstrated the proper kick. Then we all jumped in and kicked up a storm. This was real fun! Then the command was given for everyone out of the pool, so we jumped out. The next demonstration in the pool was the assistant instructor pushing off, arms out straight, and head in the water. This was called the "dead man's float." Now things were getting serious, with a name like that. It might have been that ominous name, or the fact that the air and water were cold, but twenty-five na- ked skinny boys all began to shiver. The lesson continued until our thirty minutes were up. Then we all took a hot shower and the next group of swimmers had their turn. The best part about the YMCA was the luxury of having hot showers, which I had never experienced before.

This was a hard group to teach how to swim, as we were mostly all sinkers, and floating was beyond most of us. The fifth and final day came, and we all took the swim test. We had to swim fifty feet, the length of the pool, and those who could, were rewarded with a beginner's swim pin. About twenty of us passed the test. I didn't pass the test because I could only swim the fifty feet underwater. It was the following year that I perfected swimming fifty feet on top of the water and earned my pin.

Pipe Smoking

My maternal grandfather, Daniel Hughes, smoked a pipe; in fact, he smoked several pipes. They were all made out of wood. He would knock the ashes out of the pipe, pack in new tobacco, and tamp it down with his finger. Then, with a "strike anywhere" match, he lit the pipe with a scratch of his thumbnail, applied it to the tobacco, and sucked in the smoke. When his pipe was lit, it took constant puffing to keep the fire going.

There were many brands of tobacco to choose from. Grandfather smoked "Five Brothers'," which came wrapped in a paper wrapper. My Uncle Danny, Daniel William Hughes, who lived with us during the Great Depression of the 1930's, preferred to smoke "Granger," which came in a one-quart tin can.

As a boy, I liked the smell of tobacco, but not the smoke. My Uncle Chris, Christian Jessen, smoked "corncob" pipes, which were actually made out of yellow corn cobs. My grandmother's brother, my Great Uncle Will, William Davis, also living with us in the 1930's had seven pipes; one for each day of the week. He said they tasted better with a little rest.

Most pipe smokers liked the longer wooden matches as it sometimes took a long time to get the tobacco burning. Because the pipe burned the tobacco from the top down, the puffing sometimes became a lot of sucking of air.

One of the advantages of pipe smoking was that it was cheaper than cigarettes. But the greatest advantage pipe smokers had was when they were asked a tough question. The pipe smoker could puff on the pipe while he thought up an intelligent reply. If it was a truly daunting question like: What is the meaning of life? Then the smoker could reload his pipe as a delaying tactic, as this process indicated deep thought.

Some pipe smokers kept their tobacco in a pouch. Some tobacco came in cans that could be slipped into a shirt pocket. One of these brands was called "Prince Albert," whose majestic picture was on the can. One immature joke we boys would play would be to call the tobacco store and ask, "Do you have Prince Albert in a can?" When the store owner would respond, "Yes," then we boys would shout out, "Well let him out!" and then quickly hang up the phone. The fact that the store owner always answered and did not hang up on us, leads me to believe that he liked the joke; hoping that he was talking to future tobacco customers.

The Gandy Dancer's House Fire

Before World War II, Grove Avenue in Metuchen, New Jersey, was a dirt road with a grade crossing at the Pennsylvania Railroad. On the east side of Grove Avenue and north of the railroad stood an old house. It was used by the railroad as housing for the gandy dancers. "Gandy dancer" is a slang term for the railroad track maintenance workers. One of their jobs was to keep the tracks at a proper grade. When the track was low, it was jacked up and ballast stones were driven under the ties with picks. The up and down motion of this was the gandy dance.

One day we kids were playing in the woods nearby, catching frogs and turtles in a pond. Suddenly we heard yelling and we all ran toward the old house. Behind the old house was a smaller building that was the kitchen. It was connected to the house by an enclosed hallway that also served as an eating area. The kitchen was on fire!

We all watched as the fire engines arrived. There were no

fire hydrants around so a pumper truck pulled alongside the pond we were just playing at and the firemen threw in a suction hose. The pump was started and water began to spray out onto the fire. The fire had gotten a good start, and just when it seemed the fire was under control, the pond ran dry. The flames reared back up in the kitchen, and soon the hallway went and then the old wooden house.

We all watched this sad event. The firemen picked up their hoses and the trucks rolled away. We kids went back to the pond, which now was a mud hole. Each one of us now easily caught several large bullfrogs. To carry them home, we stuffed them down our shirts. They kind of tickled as we walked home. We must have looked strange with our shirts bulging in and out as the frogs moved around. Life was great!

My mother, Hannah Hughes Jessen, had a different opinion, as all she saw was a dirty boy, in very muddy clothes, with frogs. Sometimes it is tough to be a mother.

The Hose Tower

During the 1930's, the Eagle Hook and Ladder Company was located on Main Street, Metuchen, New Jersey. It is the large red brick building at 398 Main Street. You can see their symbol embedded in the wall, an eagle. Near the back of this building was a tall wooden tower that was used for drying the canvas fire hoses.

Directly across the street, the building at 399 Main Street used to contain an ice cream store named the "Big Dip." For five cents you could get one dip, and for ten cents you could get two dips. Eating a double dip ice cream cone on a hot day took a lot of skill. The secret was to spot the drips and lick fast. Keep the cone vertical, and don't lick too hard. Dropping the ice cream on the sidewalk must be avoided at all costs.

One hot summer day, the large doors to the firehouse were open and four volunteer firemen sat in chairs leaning against the open doors. Across the street a young boy came out of the Big Dip with his single dip. Looking across the street he saw flames shooting up from the hose drying tower.

"Fire! Fire! The firehouse is on fire!" shouted the boy. The four firemen sat still, and one shouted back, "Eat your ice cream kid."

"It really is a fire," he called back. Then pieces of burning shingles started falling onto Main Street.

Now the firemen sprang into action. One quickly drove the fire truck out of the building. Others connected a fire hose to the fire hydrant that used to be in front of that building and began to put water on the fire. The fire whistle went off, and soon the other volunteer fire company in town, the Washington Hose Company, arrived to help battle the fire. There was lots of excitement, thrilling action, and soon the fire was out; but the hose drying tower was destroyed.

The boy watched, licking his cone, but in all the excitement his ice cream dropped onto the sidewalk. When things calmed down, the proprietor of the Big Dip put his arm around the boy, and ushered him into the store. Soon the boy emerged with a big double dip ice cream cone and the biggest smile on his face.

The First Spring Swim

After a few warm spring days in New Jersey during the 1930's, it was time to go for a swim in the millpond. A few boys and I walked south along the track of the gravel railroad; the connection between the Pennsylvania Railroad and the Raritan Arsenal. We walked down the tracks keeping our eyes and ears alert for any steam engines that might be coming down the tracks. We soon left Metuchen, New Jersey, and crossed over U.S. Route 1. The highway was three lanes in those days, one in each direction with the center lane used as a passing lane. It was later called the suicide lane because of so many head-on collisions.

The next section of railroad track was in the woods, and then we came to the millbrook, which drained the southeast end of Metuchen and at one time some of Metuchen's sanitary sewer waste. The old mill was long gone, but half the milldam remained on the brook and created the millpond. The water was about four feet deep and was not too cold. A large tree limb hung over the water with a rope attached.

This area was deserted so we had no need for bathing suits or towels, we just went skinny dipping. We swung out on the rope and dropped into the pond. After a refreshing swim, we air dried, got dressed, then walked back along the railroad tracks. We tried to get back home before the five o'clock fire siren called us home for dinner.

During the summer we went further south to the clay pits, south of what is now Middlesex County College. These ponds were very deep with crystal clear water. The top layer of water was nice and warm, but below was very cold water. Our parents did not know that we were swimming there, but we remembered warnings that cold water could cause cramps in swimmers, so we were very careful.

Water

The first settlers always tried to build their homes near a stream for a water supply. As soon as they could, they would dig a well.

Many years ago I watched a well digger at work. He started out selecting a site. He took a witch hazel divining rod. This was a forked "Y" shaped stick about one inch in diameter. He held it with two hands at the top of the "Y," fingers pointed in. He walked back and forth with the rod bouncing in front of him. Suddenly it pointed straight down. He passed that spot and the rod leveled out. Next he swung around at another angle and as he passed the spot the rod pointed down. He now had the well location.

I tried it but it didn't work for me. I didn't have the gift.

The soil was sandy. He started to dig. When he was down about five feet he started to build his shield. It was an open ended wooden cylinder about four feet in diameter.

The shield was put in the hole, backfilled with the sandy soil, and the inside lined with brick. Then the digging continued. A husky 16-year-old boy pulled the dirt up in a bucket. The boy also continued the brickwork up on top of the shield.

The well would be dug down in the center and then the earth was scraped out under the shield. The weight of the brick pushed it down.

At fifteen feet the well digger was knee deep in water. The pump was rigged and he dug five feet more. Then he put in a flagstone slab on top with a small hole for the pump. Job complete.

In early times, usually two wells were dug; one at the house and one at the barn. Horses, cows, and other animals drink a lot of water.

Later, masonry cisterns were built in the ground. These were usually built of brick, ten to twelve feet deep and about eight feet in diameter. They were shaped like a mason jar corbelling into a two-foot hole at the top. Rain water from the roof was led into the cistern; this meant that the water was soft.

When I was a little boy we had a cistern, a well, and city water. The well was used to water the garden. The city water cost money and was used as little as possible, primarily for drinking and cooking water. The cistern water was used for washing; both people and clothes.

There was a pitcher pump in the kitchen right over the cistern, which was located in the crawl space. Saturday night I was washed in a stone tub with water heated on the nearby coal stove. That part was great. Then I had to squat under the pitcher pump as I was rinsed off with cold water from the cistern. I still finish off my showers today with cold water.

The Edgar School

In September 1936, I was in the fifth grade at the Washington School, now the Mildred B. Moss Elementary School, in Metuchen, New Jersey. My class had forty-five pupils. There were three elementary schools: Edgar, Washington, and Franklin. During the first week of school I was moved to the Edgar School, which then had twenty-five pupils in the fifth grade. Looking back, the principal, Mrs. Moss, wanted to even out the classes. I was the only one who moved, so I guess I represented ten pupils! Incidentally, in those days students walked to school and most went home for lunch.

I was overjoyed with the move. The school was at the edge of town and behind the school was an adventure land. After school we explored a large wooded area. Past the woods was a swamp. The Middlesex County Mosquito Commission had dug a ditch to drain the swamp. I was impressed that the mosquitoes had their own commission. We would walk along the ditch and could catch some really big frogs. In those days we did not know how important it was to keep mosquito habitats and wetlands; we simply thought it was healthier for everyone to eliminate mosquitoes. Times change.

Past the drained swamp was a small brook that started from a spring. You could get down on your knees and slurp up the cool clear water. At the bottom of the spring you could see the water pushing up little volcano-shaped piles of sand.

Next was the rubber factory. This was an abandoned empty building with broken windows. Strewn inside and outside the building were hundreds of various sizes of rubber sink stoppers. During World War II, this building became Wiley's Flugent, which manufactured military flares—most with parachutes.

Last was Metuchen's town garbage dump. You would be surprised how much good stuff people throw away.

Today, all this has been replaced by Interstate 287, with nothing left but the memories.

Pea Shooters

A pea shooter is like a blow pipe that shoots peas (green cherries) instead of poison darts. You would put a pea in your mouth and blow it out of the pea shooter.

With proper tongue training you could put lots of peas in your mouth and have a multiple-shot pea shooter. NOTE! Improper tongue training could result in swallowing all your ammunition.

In the springtime, the wild cherry trees display their blossoms. Soon the blossoms change to green pea-size cherries. When I was in grade school this was harvest time for kids who were shooters like me.

Next we needed pea shooters. This required a trip to the dump of Nixon Nitration. We would start by walking the tracks of the gravel railroad. This was the single track of the Pennsylvania Railroad from Metuchen, New Jersey, south to the Raritan Arsenal. After that a walk along the Arsenal fence by the golf course. We kept our eyes peeled for golf balls since the golfers would pay twenty-five cents for each ball. Then south onto Mill Road past the flooded clay pits.

If it was warm we would stop for some skinny dipping. After swimming we walked a while as we dried off. Once we were dry we would get dressed. Then we arrived at the dump. One of Nixon Nitration's products was the barrels for plastic fountain pens. We would search the dump and find the rejected pieces. Most were twelve to eighteen inches long. We would take a good supply, for the barrels were valuable trading stuff.

Most boys took the eighteen-inch barrels. They shot further but were harder to conceal. The shorter ones could be slipped up your sleeve. The green wild cherries were just the right size. The most fun was hitting someone in the back of the neck and then calling out "Mosquitoes!"

Sometimes we would choose up sides and have pea shooter battles. Three hits and you were out. This was life for young boys before organized sports, television, computers, video games, and the Internet.

The Diving Board

When I was a kid, pools had diving boards. The Metuchen YMCA (Young Men's Christian Association) had one. The Rahway, New Jersey, public outdoor pool had a low board and a high board. Your first dive off a high board is a real heart pounder.

At the YMCA we had diving instruction. The trick was to make the springboard bounce. Match the rhythm of the board bounce so that when you took the end step the board was going down with you. This would give you the best spring.

When the instructor left we did the dives as a team. Behind the diver was the springer(s). They would work in tandem with the diver getting a good spring. One day they tried three springers and the diving board broke.

Money was tight and a new board was expensive. The broken board was taken to the East Jersey Lumber Company on Prospect Street, in Metuchen, where they had a sawmill. Their yard ran from Essex Avenue to High Street. This was full of various size logs. The choice was between red oak and white oak.

Red oak was chosen. A very large log was taken to the sawmill and a single board was cut and shaped to the board dimensions. The new board was bolted into place and covered with coco mats. The new board was a success, but we were limited to one springer.

After a few weeks, the board started to warp. The left side went up an inch or two and the right side went down. Now diving was more exciting! If you took a regular dive, the board would throw you to the right, alarmingly close to the side of the pool.

Eventually the red oak board got too exciting and money was found for a new regular springboard, with a sandpaper type top. Safety triumphed over excitement!

❧❧❧

Hardball

When I was a kid during the Great Depression there were very few organized sports except at school. When we wanted to play hardball, we met at the ball field by the Presbyterian Church for a pickup game.

Customarily the two best players would choose up sides. One fellow would throw the bat in the air and the other fellow would catch it. Then they walked their hands alternately toward the small end of the bat. The person who reached the end got first choice. If the top hand didn't have a complete grip, the test was to swing the bat three times around his head. If he did not drop the bat, then he picked first.

Usually there was only one bat and ball, and only the infield had mitts. You learned you could safely catch a fly without a mitt by a downward hand motion to absorb the velocity.

The game was over when the five o'clock fire siren blew—time to go home for supper. The game was also over if the guy who owned the bat and ball went home.

At some point in the life of the hardball, the cover would start to come off. Then the ball was wrapped with electrician's tape. This was before duct tape. The wrapping of tape made the ball heavier, less lively, and black, thereby slowing the game down.

There is the story of a commuter cutting across the outfield and asking the left fielder, "What's the score?"

The fielder answered, "Twenty-eight to zero, their favor."

The commuter said, "That sounds pretty bad."

"No it isn't," replied the fielder, "We haven't been up at bat yet!"

The House on the Hill

My Great Uncle Will's house was on the side of the mountain on Green Hill overlooking Johnstown, Pennsylvania. The uphill side of the house was even with the ground, while the wide porch on the downhill side was twelve feet off the ground. There was no running water in the house. As you approached the house from a driveway off of Frankstown Road, you passed two springs. The first one was for drinking and cooking. The second one was for washing.

A covered greenhouse on the uphill side passed you through to a fifty-foot path to the outhouse. This was a one holer which was unique, as half the initials carved on the inside were upside down. Apparently at one time in its life, the outhouse had rolled down the hill. I hope it was unoccupied. When it was reconstructed, some of the boards were put back upside down.

The house was heated with pot belly coal stoves and the cooking was done on a coal stove.

During World War I, Great Uncle Will, William Davis, bought some worked out coal mines—cheap. About thirty percent of the coal was left in the mines as pillars to hold up the ceiling. Great Uncle Will and his men "robbed" the pillars, starting at the back of the mine and working their way out.

This was a dangerous but very inexpensive way to mine the coal.

After the war Great Uncle Will and some of his brothers and sisters went to Florida for the winter. He bought lots of land cheap. During the 1920's there was a land boom in Southern Florida and Great Uncle Will did very well selling some. This was his retirement money. Johnstown in the summer and Florida in the winter—not too bad!

When we visited my maternal grandmother's family in Johnstown, we stayed at Great Aunt Alice's, Alice Davis Jones, house at 118 Johns Street next to The Point (the point where the Little Conemaugh and the Stony Creek rivers merged). Her house was one of the few in that area that had survived the Johnstown Flood of 1889. It survived because a steam locomotive swept up by the flood had landed upstream of her house and protected it.

I liked her house because it was across the street from the local baseball stadium. You could sit on her front porch roof and watch the game. Home runs often landed in her yard and I always went home with a baseball!

Pin Boys & Bowling

In the 1930's and 1940's, Metuchen, New Jersey, had four bowling alleys: two at the YMCA (Young Men's Christian Association) and two at the Masonic Temple. At the age of fourteen my hands were big enough to pick up two bowling pins with one hand. I got a job at the Masonic Temple as a "Pin Boy" one night a week in 1940.

At the impact-end of the bowling alley, ten metal rods were lifted up by pressing a treadle with your foot. The pins had holes bored in the bottom and the pin boys set the pins on the rods. Then I would jump up on the ten-inch by eighteen-inch seat on the four-inch-thick wooden divider between the alleys and pull up my feet. The rods dropped down. The pins were set.

The bowler selected a ball from the ten or twelve supplied by the Masonic Temple. Very few bowlers could afford to own their own balls. The bowler would roll the ball down the alley. After a strike or spare, the pin boy picked up the ball and shoved it down the ball return. Then, if a strike was bowled, you would reset the pins; otherwise you cleared up the "dead wood" and waited for the next ball.

The ten bowlers would start at eight o'clock in the evening and finish about ten o'clock. I would receive my pay at the end of the evening—seventy-five cents.

I would then walk down to Danfords, where there was a soda fountain. Usually I was the only customer. "A chocolate soda, please," I requested. Mr. Danford picked up the large soda glass, added a little milk, chocolate syrup, and then you heard the swishing sound of the soda squirting in. A stir with the long spoon and then a big scoop of ice cream went on top!

I handed over my ten cents and slowly consumed my soda, savoring every mouthful. "Another one, please." Another dime and a little slower prolonged enjoyment.

"Another soda only five cents, Marty," said Mr. Danford. He liked me. Life was good.

Out the door, a deep satisfying burp, and I started up Main

Street for home. Most nights the Metuchen police car pulled up—the front door opened, a voice ordered, "Get in Marty" and I was driven home. The cops knew I was tired and full of soda. They like me too! Life was real good.

Memorial Day

Memorial Day was originally called Decoration Day. It started after the Civil War when the graves of the veterans were decorated. When I was a Boy Scout in the 1940's in Metuchen, New Jersey, our scout troop, under the supervision of the American Legion Fugle Hummer Post No. 65, put flags on the veteran graves from all wars; from the American Revolution through World War I.

Most of the graves had metal flag holders for the flags. The Revolutionary War flag holders were installed by the DAR (Daughters of the American Revolution). These metal signs had the name of the veterans on them. I don't remember any from the Mexican War. The Civil War ones had the letters GAR (The Grand Army of the Republic) on them. The men from the American Legion gave us a lot of history about the wars America fought in.

My first parade was when I was only six. I was handed a flag and joined the line of march. This parade went north on Main Street and ended at Woodwild Park. My parents lost me. I wasn't supposed to be in the parade. Finally my Uncle

Andy, Andrew Jessen, found me sitting among the tall trees licking an orange Popsicle someone gave me, listening to the program.

On Main Street opposite Woodbridge Avenue at nine o'clock Memorial Day morning, 1934, there was a dedication by the DAR of the bronze plaque commemorating the Revolutionary War skirmish fought there. A firing squad fired their rifles as a salute. I learned that ejected brass cartridges could burn your fingers, even when shooting blanks!

Most of the parades ended in Memorial Park. There was a circular paved area with a memorial on one side. Opposite this was a large trophy cannon from World War I. It could hold three or four kids on the barrel. This was the best place to see the ceremonies.

I remember a few Spanish American War Veterans riding in open cars and lots of World War I veterans marching. There was usually a contingent of soldiers from the Raritan Arsenal with several trucks towing cannons.

In church we sang the Battle Hymn of the Republic. The lyrics are from a poem by Julia Ward Howe and the tune was from a song sung by Union Troops, "John Brown's body lies a-mouldering in the grave, His soul's marching on!" "His soul's," referred to soldiers fighting to end slavery. I learned a lot of history because of Memorial Day events.

Pup Tents

Camping out for the Boy Scouts in the early 1940's was strictly a local affair. There were plenty of woods around Metuchen, New Jersey, in those days. It was best to camp in Dismal Swamp in the cold weather after the frost killed the mosquitoes. Camping in South Edison at Nixon was best in the warm weather, as there were active and abandoned clay and sand pits, which were good for swimming.

For tents we had World War I surplus shelter halves. Each soldier carried one, and when two were fastened together, it made a pup tent. When we found a good campsite we pitched our tents. Small sassafras trees were chopped with our Boy Scout Plumb axe and shaped into poles and sharp stakes. We slept on the ground, usually with only a blanket. A small ditch would be dug at the drip line of the tent to keep us dry inside if it should rain. A shallow soup-bowl-shaped hole would be dug for our hip bone, to make sleeping on the hard dirt more comfortable.

We would clear a fire ring around our proposed campfire and then get lots of firewood. When we first started we would chop down small trees. This resulted in lots of work and green smoky fires. When we were more experienced, we gathered "squaw wood," small fallen trees and limbs that an Indian squaw would have carried back to her fire, with a maximum size of four inches in diameter. We trimmed them up with our axe, which gave us kindling to start the fire. We laid the logs across the fire and when they burned through, we shoved the ends in.

Cooking was mostly hot dogs and canned food placed in a small pot hung over the fire. Breakfast was bacon and eggs cooked on our mess kit frying pan. Life was good.

When it was time to go, we burned our trash. The cans were put into the fire to burn off the labels, and then they were buried. The cans rusted really fast after they were burned.

We let the fire burn out and then covered it with dirt. We left two crossed green sticks to show our campfire was out. Our motto was "leave the campsite better than you found it."

Years later I came across a dozen Indian arrowheads, and I wanted to make this campout special. Without being seen, I dropped arrowheads around the campsite, salting the area. Most arrowheads were found, and this brought great joy for the lucky Scouts who found an arrowhead. However, not all things go as planned. One boy came up to me and asked, "Why does my arrowhead have the number three painted on it?" I told him, "That was the number of rabbits the Indian killed with that arrowhead." He walked away happy, and I learned to closely check the merchandise before giving it away.

Newspapers

One way to earn money when I was a kid was to have a newspaper route, to deliver newspapers to people's homes. Usually the papers were dropped off at your house. You had a large canvas bag with a strap that went over your shoulder and you walked along and chucked newspapers onto front yards. Once a week you would collect money from your customers. This was good business experience. If the customer did not pay you, you still had to pay for the newspapers; therefore, you lost. Many boys learned valuable business lessons like keep your customers happy, and avoid bad customers.

During the rapid business expansion that started with the outbreak of World War II in Europe, it was difficult to get men to run the newsboy operation. So home delivery stopped for the war, and people had to go to the newspaper store to buy the daily paper.

When I was fourteen years old I got a job at the newspaper store on Main Street, Metuchen, New Jersey. The newspapers came into town by train. There was a baggage car at the front of the train, and as the train pulled into town, mail and newspapers were thrown off. At seven o'clock in the morning, I would pick up the bundles of newspapers and take them to the store. Each newspaper was in its own bundle. In those days there were many different newspapers that published daily papers.

I particularly did not enjoy Thursdays and Sundays as they were "fat days," because the newspapers had so many extra pages on those days. I would need a hand truck or a wagon to move them. The bundles were tied with a rope, and sometimes I needed my pocketknife to cut the rope and make smaller piles so I could lift all the papers.

Usually each section of the paper had its own bundle. The sections would be put together at the store. *The New York Times* was the biggest and thickest newspaper. Some parts of the Sunday paper came in on Saturday, the rest came Sunday morning. There were many sections to put together. We had a long table to set section piles on. You would take one section from each pile and slide them into the front section. I probably walked half a mile inside the store putting the newspapers together.

One Sunday the sports section of the newspaper was missing. I found out what was most important to American newspaper readers. The telephone rang constantly with people looking for the missing sports section.

Sometimes the train was late, and I would sit on the baggage wagon with the man from the post office. He would have bags of mail to put on the train. Some trains did not stop at the station and he showed me how the bags would be picked up by a mail car. The bag was hung on a post, and a hook on the mail car would snatch the bag as the train roared through the station. Inside the mail car, the mail would be sorted, and dropped off at the appropriate town. I thought that was pretty neat.

My Job in the Paper Store

In 1940, I was hired to help out in a newspaper store on Main Street. My pay was four dollars and fifty cents per week for two hours a day, seven days a week. For a fourteen-year-old boy this was a fortune.

The newspaper store had a liquor store next door with a ten-foot opening between the stores. One of my duties was to put the glass beer bottles turned in for the deposit into cases.

When I arrived at work in the morning, the back room was wall to wall empty bottles with a narrow trail to the back door. To this day, when I smell stale beer, I remember straining to get the highest case on the top of the pile.

I learned something about the liquor business. A government agency called the ABC (Alcohol Beverage Control) set the selling prices. When the distributor wanted to give a break to the store owner, he would indicate the number of "broken" bottles that could be taken back for credit. When this happened, I would be given two or three bottles to take to the back room. I would take each bottle, put it inside a sock, hold it over a bucket, and hit the bottom with a hammer. The purpose of the sock was to keep the broken glass from falling into the liquor that landed in the bucket. The neck of the bottle with the unbroken tax stamp had to be returned to receive the credit.

I would be sent out to find discarded liquor bottles, particularly pints. On the corner of Main Street and Middlesex Avenue was the Methodist Church of Metuchen, New Jersey. The Methodists were against drinking and for some reason a lot of outdoor drinkers liked throwing their empty bottles there.

I would wash the bottles, pour the liquor from the bucket into the bottles, and put a cork in it. These were sold to some of our daily customers at a discount.

Sometimes on my way home, I would come across one of our steady customers having trouble getting up the stairs at the railroad station. He would grab the handrail on one side and me on the other and together we would climb the stairs. He always gave me a "Thank you very much."

Due to the blue laws that were originally designed to enforce the religious observance of Sunday as a day of worship or rest, liquor was not sold on Sundays. Sometimes when I arrived on Sunday morning to work on the newspapers, the drunks would come around, begging to be sold a bottle. As a teenage boy, this was a true learning experience and drinking alcohol didn't look like a good idea to me.

CHAPTER 3

World War II

The Raritan Arsenal

L iving through the Great Depression, most of us were very poor, but our poverty ended because of World War II, when prosperity returned. The military enlisted most of the young men and jobs were plentiful, resulting in very few unemployed workers.

Established in 1917 for World War I, the Raritan Arsenal (Raritan Center and Middlesex County College today) was a three-thousand-two-hundred-acre site located in Raritan Township, New Jersey, and bordering the Raritan River. The Arsenal contained warehouses, magazines, railroad tracks, housing, administrative buildings, and a hospital. When I was sixteen, I found out that the Arsenal had started hiring high school students part-time.

I applied for a job and got it. Fifty-six cents an hour for a skinny kid was a fortune. Of course there were a lot of skinny kids back then.

After bouncing around on several jobs I ended up in the shipping department at W-2 Warehouse. Ordinance main-tenance supplies came in by railroad and mostly went out by railroad. I was the only kid working in this warehouse and everyone called me "Junior."

The warehouse worked two shifts, seven days a week. While going to Metuchen High School, I usually worked two or three weekdays from four o'clock in the afternoon to ten o'clock in the evening, and then the day shift on Saturdays and Sundays—racking up thirty to forty hours for the week.

During summer vacation I could work fifty to sixty hours a week. I discovered what time-and-a-half overtime meant.

One day at quitting time, the word was put out that they needed workers in the ammunition area to load artillery shells. To me this was more overtime, so I volunteered.

The next day I was thinking about my big paycheck. When I arrived at work, the secretary found me and said, "Junior, report to Lieutenant Larken right away and it's not good."

I went to his office thinking I was going to be praised for helping to load the ammunition late last night. Instead he started shouting at me, "Junior what the *expletive, expletive*, do you think you are doing? Have you never heard of the child labor laws?"

I never had and stood there speechless. In my mind I was just doing my part to help win the war. "Junior, work no more than forty hours a week, no more than eight hours a day, do not work after ten o'clock in the evening, *and*, stay out of the ammunition areas." That is how I found out that I had violated the child labor laws.

The Addressograph

During World War II, while still in high school, I worked as a part-time government employee in a warehouse at the Raritan Arsenal shipping ordinance supplies. One of the things we shipped were bales of cotton waste, the size of a hay bale.

The cotton waste was used to clean the mechanical parts of the big guns used in the war. Each bale required a shipping tag held on with wires. When a boxcar was shipped out it contained hundreds of tags, which the office staff had typed.

I reported for work one day after school and my boss Leo met me and said, "Come with me Junior." He had a toolbox and gave me one to carry too. We walked up to the headquarters building, showed our picture badges to the guard, and walked in. Leo walked into an office and set his toolbox next to a young lady's desk. She opened a desk drawer. Leo opened his toolbox, pulled out a box of candy, and placed it in the drawer. I was impressed—a box of candy was hard to get during the war because of rationing. Then the three of us went down to the basement. She unlocked a padlocked door and we went in. A sign over the door read, "Authorized Personnel Only."

In this room was the addressograph, a desk-sized machine that printed addresses from metal plates. The lady showed me how this machine worked. What would take hours to type could now be stamped out in minutes. There was a heavy-duty typewriter to make the metal plates. Leo produced a box of shipping tags from my toolbox. While I worked on the tags, Leo fixed the lock on the double-hung window so it could not lock. We left with our printed tags in the toolbox.

Every time a big shipment of bales was going out, I went to the headquarters building at night, entered the basement through the rear window, and printed the tags.

This went on for months. Then one night, I opened the window to leave, put my box of tags outside on the lawn, and suddenly there were two shinny brown combat boots right in front of my face. Two strong hands jerked me through the window. As I met the guard, I told him what I was doing and showed him the tags. He said, "We are going to see the captain." I replied, "Let me close the window because you know this is a security area."

At guard headquarters I told my story to the captain. Soon my boss Leo and his boss Lieutenant Larkin arrived, who showed the captain a copy of a letter that was his request to use the addressograph. The captain said, "This was six months ago and no answer yet." As the discussion went on, it got louder and louder with many expletives. I stepped outside the room.

Finally we went back to the warehouse with our tags. The next week Leo told me everything was OK. The captain had found our letter, it was in the works, and we would be approved shortly. For many months after that I still printed the tags by climbing through the basement window—as the authorization did not arrive.

I learned a lot:

1 - When entering someplace you are not supposed to be, look like you belong. Carrying a toolbox is good. I have found a clipboard works well too.

2 - A box of candy in the right place can do wonders.

3 - Government paperwork moves very slowly, and sometimes not at all.

4 - If you can't use the front door, try the rear window.

5 - When you are a mouse in a room full of elephants, stay out of the way.

The Italian Prisoners

During World War II, while still in high school, I worked at the Raritan Arsenal. The Arsenal consisted of many warehouses on the upper level and some ordinance repair facilities. The lower level was the magazine area where ammunition was stored.

One section of the magazine area was built for World War I. These magazines were above ground structures, consisting of hollow tile walls on a concrete slab and a wooden roof. The new sections—built for World War II—were reinforced concrete, covered with earth, with only the end exposed for access.

There was no smoking allowed in the magazine area. Matches, lighters, and cigarettes were not permitted. Everyone was checked carefully before entering.

At the Arsenal were several hundred Italian prisoners of war, who had been captured in North Africa. They lived in an army barracks and they wore their army uniforms, which were dark blue in color.

They had volunteered to work and they were paid. Most of their jobs were loading and unloading freight cars. The prisoners were divided into squads of eight or ten with a United States military armed guard.

The Italian prisoners talked to some of our people who understood Italian. They were surprised at their treatment. Clean beds, hot showers, and food they had never dreamed of. A few said they wanted to escape and marry so they could live in this land of plenty.

A squad of Italian prisoners was working in the magazine area loading shells into a freight car from a World War I magazine. There was a terrific explosion! No one knows what happened. All the prisoners in the squad were killed. The force of the explosion broke windows in nearby Sayreville, New Jersey!

When I visited the site days later, all that was left of the magazine was the concrete slab. The rest was blown to smithereens. On the railroad track in front of the magazine were the wheels of the freight car. That was all that was left!

This was a very sobering experience for a sixteen year old who had casually been loading shells only a few weeks before.

The American Legion Building

The American Legion building on Lake Avenue in Metuchen, New Jersey, was once a temporary school building on the former Franklin School site. There used to be screw holes in the floor where the desks were fastened in place. In the old days desks were set in immovable rows. Books were stored in a wide slot under the desk. There was a groove carved into the desktop for a pencil, and the upper grades also had an inkwell. If the girl who sat in front of you had pigtails, the temptation to dip one pigtail in the ink was powerful, but I resisted.

After World War I, the building was moved to its present

location on Lake Avenue. The lawn in front of the building contained lots of "war trophies": a large cannon, several large-caliber trench mortars, and many large artillery shells. In front of the entrance was a large cannonball almost two feet in diameter.

At Memorial Park was another cannon in front of the old plaza (the cannon has since been removed). The annual Memorial Day parade always ended there, and it was a race among the boys to see who got to sit astride the cannon barrel. The cannon could hold four or five boys and turned out to be the best seat in the park to see the ceremonies.

During World War II all these metal war trophies were scrapped for the war effort. Today the American Legion proudly displays on its front lawn two thirty-seven-millimeter guns, with one of them fully restored.

The American Legion Fugle Hummer Post No. 65 sponsored Boy Scout Troop 14, where I was a member. The large room made a fine place for thirty or more boys to work off their enthusiasm. They also sponsored a drum and bugle corps. It was lots of fun to march in the parades down Main Street, stopping under the railroad bridge and pounding away different beats on the drums. The acoustics under the bridge were fantastic!

About this time another war trophy turned up. Inside a box hidden under the porch of the American Legion Building was a long forgotten World War I war prize—one hundred German military belt buckles, still wrapped in paper. I don't think any of the legionaries knew that they were hidden there. This treasure was shared among the legionnaires.

The buckles were stamped with the German words "Gott mit uns" which means God with us. Interestingly similar buckles were made for World War II German soldiers with a swastika on them, and the words "Gott mit uns."

The American Legion has served veterans for many years. They have also served the community in many ways and are an important part of our community fabric.

U-Boats off the Coast

Just after the Japanese Pearl Harbor attack on 7 December 1941, Germany and Italy declared war on the United States. Our military was in bad shape. Congress had cut funding past the bone.

The story was told of draftees at Fort Dix, New Jersey, training with wooden sticks for guns. In a mock battle one trainee shot another by saying, "Bang, bang, you're dead." The other trainee replied, "You can't shoot me, I'm a tank." Congress had made our military a minor threat in Hitler's eyes.

The German attack on the United States was with U-boats (submarines) off our coasts, attacking all shipping between American ports and all shipping to our ally England.

Coastal shipping from the south, particularly crude oil from Texas and Louisiana headed for New Jersey refineries, came by way of the Intracoastal Waterway to Delaware Bay. From there the ships had to go out to sea off the coast of New Jersey—where they were in grave danger—in order to get to New York Harbor.

The German U-boats were just off shore, and these ships made easy targets, particularly at night when they were silhouetted against the lights of the shore communities. There was local resistance to turning off these lights.

When the sinkings began, the beaches were covered with black crude oil, debris from the wrecks, and even dead bodies. This got everyone's attention. One Sunday, my father drove our family down to the New Jersey shore, and we saw crude oil, ship debris, and empty cork life jackets strewn over the sand.

A "brown out" was begun. Street lights were painted black on the ocean side. Advertising signs were turned off and window shades pulled down.

Larger fishing boats with one depth charge and a machine gun patrolled off shore with little effect. Later, destroyers with sonar appeared and later still blimps from Lakehurst Naval Air Station. The cargo ship losses were kept out of the newspapers, but many people knew.

I remember hearing the adults talking about it. This was the era when children were seen but not heard.

Many adults wondered why Congress spent so much money paying farmers not to grow food and not enough on national defense. These farm subsidies were started during the Great Depression to keep the farmers in business.

During the Great Depression, when driving around New Jersey, my family had seen potato fields where the ripened potatoes had been dug up, strung in a row on the ground, and covered with a poison green dye so people couldn't eat them!

Remember we won that war, but in the beginning we were losing; especially in the North Atlantic and the Western Pacific.

Airplane Spotting

D uring World War II, we had a volunteer airplane spotting post in Metuchen, New Jersey. Originally it was in Raritan Township over by the Raritan Arsenal on Woodbridge Avenue east of Main Street. Shortly after it started, it was moved to Metuchen, north of East Chestnut Avenue and east of Linden Avenue. This was the time when America began participating in the war and we were losing on all fronts. We thought the government was worried about enemy airplanes, so we citizens had to help Uncle Sam.

The spotting post was a two-story octagonal-shaped observation building. The first floor was to be a lavatory and office but this was never finished. The sanitary facilities were in the surrounding brush covered fields. The second floor had a center glassed-in office with a telephone and a four-foot-wide walkway around the outside.

Two observers manned the post for two-hour shifts, day and night. When any airplane came into sight, it would be reported by telephone. The airplane would be identified by engine type (single, bi-motor, or tri-motor), height (low or high), bearing, and course. Our post code name was Elliot One Nine.

As a Boy Scout I usually took two shifts a week. There was an older man who also took two shifts. A lot of people were a little afraid of him as they said he was grouchy.

I was asked to partner up with him and not knowing any better I said, "Yes." It turned out my new partner was a naturalist. We talked about birds, insects, and trees, and I learned a lot. The time would fly by as he was very nice and was a natural teacher. For example, did you know that you can tell the temperature by counting the chirps of a cricket? The warmer it gets the quicker the cricket chirps.

In foul weather we could not see any airplanes, so we would report based on the airplanes we heard. I don't think the government was worried about enemy German airplanes later on. They were more interested in keeping track of our own airplanes, and we volunteers helped keep Metuchen safe.

High School Shop

When I went to Metuchen High School in the early 1940's, the girls took a class called domestic science, where they learned to cook and sew. The boys took wood shop. They learned about tools and how to make things. For instance, a crosscut saw has triangular teeth like the bottom half of an "X." A ripsaw's teeth are like the bottom half of a capital "R." Crosscut saws cut across the grain of the wood. Ripsaws cut parallel to the grain.

We learned to use power tools: drill presses, planers, and table saws. Each of us had projects, usually some sort of furniture. I made a walnut coffee table. It was a lot of work, especially the finish, which required hand sanding and varnishing. Currently, the table supports a glass cage with my granddaughter Katharine's pet gecko living inside.

In my senior year, I had a slight accident at home on a planer. I cut a very slight nick in the tips of two fingers. This ruined my career as a violinist. I had played the violin in the high school orchestra since seventh grade. I started out as second violin and ended my orchestra career as second violin. The second violinists usually didn't play the melody. Apparently, the conductor thought I was very good at not playing the melody.

When the war started, all high school shop classes throughout the nation began making scale models of our airplanes and enemy airplanes. These were made from raw wood and shaped by hand. Our group was assigned English bombers. I made a Halifax bomber—the model had a wingspan of about eight inches. They were painted flat black.

These models were used in aircraft recognition classes by the Armed Forces. The idea was for gunners and fighter pilots to identify friend or foe correctly and, thereby, reduce "friendly fire."

So even in high school shop class, we felt like this was another way all of us were helping in the war effort.

The Navy Physical

In January 1944, as a senior in high school, I volunteered to join the United States Naval Reserve. I was seventeen years of age and had my parents' permission, but I looked much younger. I had to go to New York City to Grand Central Palace for a physical. This was where the automobile show was held; it was a big building.

Upon entering I was told to strip down and put my clothes in a box. As I handed my box in, a sailor said, "Give me your hand." I stuck out my hand and he wrote a number on it. "That's your box number so you get the right clothes back," he explained. "Now go through the double door, follow the line, and keep your papers in your right hand."

I entered the huge area; there were several hundred naked men there. Medical personnel were stationed along the line with examiners and one person to fill out the findings on my paper in my right hand. Everything was well organized. As an instrument was pushed into each ear, a technician said, "We are just checking to see if the light goes through."

There were basically two groups being examined. First were the volunteers who wanted to pass. Second were those men being drafted. By 1944, most of the obvious men, who were good soldier material, were in the service already. Now they were down to older men, most with wives and children. These men were reluctant to go to war, since they had families to support. They were looking for any way to fail the physical examination.

I wanted to pass and was doing real well until I got to the psychological exam. There were two beat-up desks, side to side, with a steel chair facing each examiner. I sat down on the steel chair—it was cold against my bare bottom. This was not good. The questioning then started.

"Do you like girls?" asked the psychologist. "Yes," I answered. Then he asked about my preferences, about high school, and other things. Finally he said, "I am going to reject you because you are too young. Maybe in six or eight months you could try again."

I was crestfallen. "That's not fair! I'll get older in the Navy," I pleaded.

The psychologist at the adjoining desk looked up and said, "Let me talk to the kid."

I walked around to his desk. A big guy was just getting up from the seat. I sat on the steel chair—it was nice and warm. Things were looking up!

The second psychologist asked why I chose the Navy. I told him. Then he asked, "Can you tie any knots?" "Yes," I answered. He pulled open a desk drawer, took out a piece of clothes line, and told me to tie a knot. I put my hands *behind* my back, tied a knot, and showed him.

"What knot is this and what is it used for?" he asked. I replied, "It's called a masthead knot. It is used to rig a mast in a small boat. The front loop goes to the forestay, the side loops go to the port and starboard sidestays, and the ends go to the backstay."

He carefully put the knot back in the drawer, signed my papers, and said, "You'll do."

Masthead Knot

Boot Camp and the Flying Five

I n late June 1944 at the innocent age of seventeen, I, along with the other sailors on our train from New York City, arrived at Great Lakes Naval Training Center on Lake Michigan, north of Chicago, Illinois, at approximately twenty hundred hours (2000, eight o'clock in the evening). We were fed a dinner of hot leftovers and sent to various barracks. These were very large barracks with wooden bunks stacked three high, which housed newly arrived recruits who were yet to be assigned to their regiment. I went in the door of the barracks and was told, "Your bunk is number seventy-six."

I was halfway through trying to find my way to my bunk when they turned the lights off! Now I was lost in the dark in an unfamiliar place full of men who wanted to sleep.

I fumbled around with only enough light to tell if a bunk was occupied. If the occupant of a bunk was not snoring, I assumed he was awake and I would ask him his bunk number. By trial and error I finally found bunk seventy-six, which fortunately was a middle bunk.

The next day I was given an envelope full of papers and sent to various stations to be physically examined. Again my eyes, ears, mouth, etc. were being looked at as I went from person to person and notes were written on my paperwork.

The next day, one hundred and nineteen potential sailors and I were taken to a building with a big room with lines drawn on the floor that outlined one hundred and twenty approximately five-foot-square boxes. We were all told to go stand in one of the squares on the floor. In each square was a cardboard box and lid. We were told to take off our clothes and put them, along with our wallets and any other personal items, into the boxes, and to write our home address on the box lid. When we were done there were one hundred and twenty potential sailors standing naked in a large room with everything they had brought with them to boot camp in a cardboard box addressed to their home. As I left this room, I looked back at the one hundred and twenty lonely boxes, left behind, as I thought of what my new life would be like.

In the next room we were given a cotton mattress cover, which I thought was just a big bag. We walked past a very long counter where storekeepers stuffed our mattress cover with shoes, socks, underwear ("skivvies"), white uniform, navy blue uniforms, dungarees, pea coat, caps, hats, pillow cover, and towels. We all quickly got dressed into our new dungarees.

After putting our name tag on our bag, we threw it onto a truck and marched off in our new shoes to our new home—the barracks. It was a two-story building with one hundred and twenty double bunks on each floor (deck). We were assigned a bunk number. Each bunk contained a new mattress, pillow, blanket, canvas hammock, and sea bag.

The next two hours were spent stenciling our names on our gear, rolling each piece of clothing into a roll, and tying it with a string (a "stop"). These rolled clothes were then stowed into our sea bags, which were tied up ("triced") to a four-by-four rail that divided the rows of bunks. If the rolling was done properly, even the dress blues came out wrinkle free.

Next was a trip to the barber shop. Ten barbers quickly scalped one hundred and twenty heads. Most of us already had crew cuts, as long hair was very rare for men in those days.

Finally we marched off to the mess hall for some lunch. A big sign announced, "*Take* ALL YOU WANT—BUT—*Eat* <u>ALL</u> You TAKE." Today, new recruits mostly lose weight in boot camp, but we all gained weight!

Then it was announced that today was payday. I thought things were getting better all the time. Our Company #1448 marched to the ship's service building. Entering alphabetically in single file, we were given a pay voucher for five dollars and told to sign it. We then walked up to the dispersing officer—an ensign with a Colt .45-caliber automatic pistol resting on his desk. I thought, "Nobody is going to rob him." I handed him my signed voucher, and he handed me a five dollar bill. As I walked down the line, the next guy took away my five dollar bill and handed me a canvas bag ("ditty" bag). The next sailor gave me one dollar and twenty-five cents and said, "Your change." That is why they called it "the flying five." You had five dollars in your hand and two steps later it was gone.

The bag contained personal essentials: toothbrush, Pepsodent toothpaste, Barbasol shaving cream, razor, razor blades, shoe polish, brush, pencils, and writing paper. We also received the 1943 edition of *The Bluejackets' Manual*, the "Bible" for Navy personnel that described everything all enlisted men should know about the Navy. The Navy thought of everything.

I joined the Navy because it was so neat and clean. I was soon to find out just who kept it so neat and clean!

The Regimental Bugler

On 11 September 2009, the family was at Newport, Rhode Island, for the graduation of my grandson, Johnathan Jessen, from Officer Candidate School, where he was commissioned an ensign in the United States Navy. Because I had been an officer in the Navy during the Korean War, I was allowed to swear him in at a private ceremony. I was all choked up.

Then we went to a large drill hall to hear a very good speech from the 75th Secretary of the Navy, Ray Mabus, and others. The graduating company was standing "at ease" for all the speeches. After a half hour, I noticed two Marines standing behind these newest Navy officers. Then suddenly one man collapsed. The Marines carried him out to another room. Soon a second man hit the deck, and he too was carried out by the Marines. This brought back memories when I was a sailor during World War II.

It was at the Great Lakes Naval Training Center, located on Lake Michigan north of Chicago, Illinois—boot camp. I was a company drummer and part of the regimental drum and bugle corps. It was a hot sunny day in July 1944 and time for Saturday inspection. The head of the corps called me out of formation and said, "Jessen, the bugler split his lip. You are to take his place." "Aye aye, sir," was my response.

I got a bugle and went to the head of the formation. I knew just what to do. There were ten companies of one hundred and twenty men each, lined up. My job was to go ahead of the inspecting party and blow "attention" as each company was approached.

At the first company I blew "attention" and they snapped to. When the inspection was finished I blew "carry on," and then went to the next company. It was so hot that day, but I was feeling very perky. When I blew "attention" for the fifth company, they snapped to and one of the sailors in the front row pitched forward and landed flat on his face. Soon there were about thirty sailors in various stages of collapse. I was really shook up. What did I do wrong?

The medical corpsmen arrived with wet towels and gradually order was restored. The senior inspecting officer walked up to me and put his arm around my shoulder and gave me a squeeze. I was really nervous now. In a soft voice he whispered in my ear, "It wasn't your fault, son. They had just gotten their yellow fever shots. Now let's move on to the next company."

The Grease Pit

After boot camp in the fall of 1944, other sailors and I were transported by train from the Great Lakes Naval Training Center to attend the sixteen-week quartermaster school at the United States Naval facility at Bainbridge, Maryland.

A quartermaster's duties are to stand the deck and bridge watches, help with navigation, steer the ship, take bearings and soundings, plot courses, and keep the quartermaster's notebook from which the ship's log book is written. At quartermaster school we were trained in the use of navigation instruments, on how to interpret weather messages, the use of tide and current tables, and how to read charts to determine the ship's position. In addition we needed to know signaling, including semaphore, flag hoists, and flashing light signals.

About one hundred sailors who had just arrived were lined up alphabetically for work details. I stood next to Seaman First Class Bruce S. Jacobs, who was built like a Mack truck. He was big, tough, and he had a mean-looking face. When only four sailors were left, the chief strolled over to Jacobs and growled, "You guys are going to the mess hall to work in the grease pit."

The chief took us to the grease pit. It was a room about twenty feet long by fifteen feet wide with long wide shelves on one side. The shelves were built with two by two inch slats that held up large serving pans. Also there were rectangular five-gallon stainless steel containers to fit in the steam table that we called gunboats. The other side of the room had two large sinks, with a long steel counter equipped with shower hoses for rinsing.

The crew we were replacing was finishing the breakfast cleanup. Some trays and gunboats were on the shelves, but most were on the floor. The sailors were elbow deep in hot soapy water. Their hands and arms were white and their skin looked like it was losing a battle with the strong soap. The floor was covered with a greasy, slimy, gunk.

We took over with the chief giving us instruction. After hours of hard work we were exhausted and finished. Just then a dozen mess cooks came in and started taking out the clean pans and gunboats for lunch. Once again the floor was quickly covered with dirty pans and gunboats and we had to start washing all over again. The supper meal was a repeat of lunch. It was eleven o'clock at night when we finally finished cleaning up.

The next morning Jacobs was mumbling, "I've got to fix this. I've got to fix this." As the mess cooks came in to pick up the pans and gunboats Jacobs told them, "Do not bring the pans and gunboats back. Just fill them up with the same thing." A few challenged this decision, but Jacobs stared them down. Then a cook came in to complain. Jacobs invited him outside to discuss the problem. Jacobs came back smiling saying, "Everything is OK."

We ended up only washing one-quarter of what we did the day before and we had extra time. So Jacobs had us clean the greasy floor and by the next day everything in the grease pit sparkled.

Saturday came and we were told there would be a captain's inspection but not to worry; he never comes into the grease pit. This gave us a couple of hours to rest. So we took the gunboats off the shelves and stretched out on the shelves to take a nap.

Suddenly there was a shout, "Attention on deck!" We jumped off of our shelves and stood at attention. There stood the captain, who looked at the gunboats on the floor and then looked at us. The executive officer, standing behind him, having seen us sleeping on the shelves said, "I will see that these men are punished, sir."

The captain replied, "Not at all. I have never seen this place so clean. You men go back up on the shelves, go back to sleep. Well done!"

The Troop Train

In mid-March 1945, my United States Navy quartermaster class was being moved from Bainbridge, Maryland, to Camp Shoemaker, a United States Naval Training and Personnel Distribution Center, twenty-eight miles east of Oakland, California, for assignment overseas.

The sailors had their sea bags packed with their hammock wrapped around it and lashed properly. We marched down to the railhead to board the train, which would take five days to cross the country. Good news! We were told that we would be traveling in the top luxury of the day—a Pullman. When we arrived the train was waiting for us, and, instead of luxury railcars, it was ordinary boxcars with the word "Pullman" lettered on the sides. Inside were bunks stuffed as tightly as possible, three rows high.

I was in the boxcar next to the kitchen car. The cook with his dirty white apron strolled in and asked, "Any of you guys want to help in the kitchen car?" The rule in the Navy was to never volunteer. But I volunteered anyway.

The cook told us that the troops would only get two meals a day. Breakfast would be scrambled eggs and oatmeal cereal, and supper would be sandwiches. The volunteers made lots of sandwiches. The sandwiches had to have two slices of meat (salami, baloney, or ham) and butter. We had a hand-operated slicer and we had to cut the meat as thin as possible. The test was to lay a slice on a newspaper and you had to be able to see the newsprint. Not read it, just see it. The butter had to be one narrow swipe of a knife. The good news was that the volunteers ate all day long.

When the train arrived at the West Coast, the sailors were marched away. The cook left the train carrying boxes of steaks, butter, and much, much more. Wartime was a period of food rationing, and the cook was leaving with a considerable load of valuable merchandise.

It was an education for me to see how one evil man could steal from so many men in order to enrich himself. I guess that is why they called him, "The Belly Robber."

The Beer Mystery

On 26 April 1945, my quartermaster school section 721 boarded the troop transport USS *General M. B. Stewart* (AP-140) in San Francisco, California, for a twenty-eight-day voyage to the Philippines. There were over three thousand Naval personnel as passengers aboard the ship, commanded by Captain M. C. Heine. The majority of the Naval personnel were enlisted teenagers of the Naval Reserve who had just reached enlistment or draft age. The rest were older Naval personnel who had been drafted when the draft age upper limit had been raised. For the most part there were no troops in their twenties.

My bunk was in a very large sleeping compartment that had an access hole to a cofferdam. A cofferdam is a compartment about four feet wide running athwartship with a steel bulkhead fore and aft.

The supply officer had several truckloads of bottled beer to deliver to the Philippines. The cofferdam was the perfect place to store it safely. The access hole was covered with an elliptical plate about two feet by three feet. It was bolted down with twenty bolts.

After the beer cases were loaded in San Francisco, the bolts were tightened with a big wrench and the supply officer put four paper tapes across the plate in an "X" shape and signed his name on each tape. Every day hundreds of troops walked past the plate with the signed paper tape seals. During the voyage, the supply officer would periodically inspect the plate to make sure that the paper tape seals with his name on them had not been broken.

When we reached our destination, Guiuan Roadstead, Samar Island in the Philippines, the supply officer removed the untouched signed paper tapes, unscrewed the bolts, and then removed the plate. The cofferdam was empty! The only things left were broken wooden beer cases and pieces of metal strapping. What happened to the bottled beer?

The mystery was solved when the supply officer went inside the cofferdam with a flashlight. After close inspection he discovered that a hole had been cut in the bulkhead from the deck below.

Unknown culprits had removed the beer and shared it with their co-conspirators and friends. There was no problem drinking the beer. After each bottle of beer was consumed, the empty glass bottle had been thrown overboard.

An inspection of the cofferdam bulkhead from the deck below did not show any holes! After the beer was removed, the hole had been welded back up and painted over. The new paint was not noticed because all the paint aboard the ship was new since the ship had just been commissioned in San Francisco on 3 March 1945. The only evidence to solve the mystery was the unpainted patch on the *inside* of the cofferdam.

I think it was the United States Navy Seabees who did it. Fourteen Navy enlisted men of the 502nd Naval Construction Battalion (CB) maintenance unit were quartered on the deck below my bunk. It was the perfect crime. Six days earlier on 16 May 1945, they had disembarked the ship in Manus, Admiralty Islands. The Seabees were over two thousand nautical miles away from the crime scene when it was detected!

The Latrine

In 1945, the Philippine Islands were a staging area for the invasion of Okinawa, Japan. Huge tent cities were constructed for the soldiers. Sanitation was handled by outdoor latrines. The officers' latrine was a four holer. It was a substantial building with a sloping roof, wooden sides on the bottom half, and screening on the top half for ventilation and to keep the flies away.

A deep hole was dug and the latrine was placed over it. When the hole was full, a new hole was dug and the latrine was moved over it. The used hole was mounded over with dirt, and a sign was installed, "LATRINE # 74-6 CLOSED 10 MAY 1945."

In order to extend the life of each location, the waste paper was set on fire once a week. One day the latrine orderly swept the floor, added the toilet paper, sprinkled gasoline into the pit, and closed all the lids.

Unfortunately, he checked and discovered he had no matches. He hung a sign on the latrine door saying "CLOSED" and went searching for matches. Smoking a cigarette, a second lieutenant came along, ignored the sign, and went in to use the facility. When he finished his smoke, he opened the lid next to him, and flipped in the cigarette butt.

Witnesses reported hearing a muffled explosion followed by seeing the lieutenant come flying out the door. Fortunately, his only injury was some singed body hair and wounded dignity. The latrine proceeded to burn to the ground. The next sign read, "LATRINE # 74-7 BURNED 21 MAY 1945, BURIED 22 MAY 1945, REST IN PEACE!"

The Mission

During World War II, I was once on a Philippine Island called Samar awaiting assignment to a ship or permanent island duty. I was given temporary quarters in a pyramid tent at Navy Base #3149 on the edge of a coral airstrip, adjacent to the jungle in Guiuan, Samar.

The United States Navy always keeps you working, so I was assigned the job of jeep driver to a legal officer. I was a "go for"; go for this, go for that, while I awaited assignment.

In my travels I noticed that every morning at 1000 hours (ten o'clock in the morning), an Army Air Force P-38 fighter plane took off. I visualized it strafing Japanese positions, shooting down Japanese Zeros (long range carrier-based fighter aircraft operated by the Imperial Japanese Navy Air Service), or perhaps on a vital photo reconnaissance mission.

One day I had to pick up some paperwork from the airfield control tower, so I asked, "What mission is in store for the P-38 today?" The response was, "Oh! That is the daily flight to freeze the ice cream for the officers' club."

My Ship Comes In

The date was 18 June 1945 and I was a Seaman First Class due to depart from the Western Pacific Island of Morotai, Netherlands East Indies (Indonesia today). My sea bag was packed full of clothing, with my hammock, mattress, blanket, and pillow all lashed to the outside. It weighed about one hundred pounds and at eighteen years of age, I weighed just a little more! A small boat, an LCVP (Landing Craft Vehicle Personnel), pulled up to the dock and I jumped in with twenty-one other alphabetically assigned Naval Reservists, including Seaman First Class Bruce Jacobs from quartermaster school.

Ahead of us, anchored in the harbor was our ship, the USS *Albert T. Harris*, a *John C. Butler*-class destroyer escort, DE number 447. Built at Federal Shipbuilding & Dry Dock

Company, Port Newark, New Jersey, she was commissioned on 29 November 1944, with Lieutenant Commander Sidney King in command. She was 306 feet long and 36 feet 8 inches at the beam, with five-inch gun turrets fore and aft. The ship bristled with twenty-millimeter and forty-millimeter anti-aircraft guns. Outfitted with the most advanced SU (surface) radar, SA (air) radar, and sonar, the ship also had depth charges and hedge-hogs (an anti-submarine weapon developed by the British Royal Navy during World War II).

Destroyer escorts were originally designed in response to the German submarine attacks on supply convoys off the Atlantic coast and between the United States and Great Britain. Their specifications called for standardized engines and equipment so they could be built quickly. They were small, highly maneuverable warships designed to search, locate, and *destroy* submarines. In addition, they were designed to *escort* and protect ship convoys, hence the name "destroyer escort."

I climbed aboard, saluted the colors and the officer of the deck. He took my papers and assigned a boatswain's mate to show me to my bunk. The bunks were stacked three high, with pipe frames and a canvas bottom laced around the edges. I was given the middle bunk on the starboard side of the after sleeping compartment next to the hull of the ship. On the ship's deck under the lowest bunk were three metal lockers. He pointed which would be mine—the middle locker.

An old chief had told me, "When you get on board your ship, find your bunk, find the head (naval talk for the bathroom), find the chow line, and then your assigned station." I accomplished all of that as I climbed up to the ship's bridge, my assigned station for general quarters, and reported to Quartermaster Second Class Charles E. Blackstone.

Quartermaster Blackstone asked me about my training, and then explained, "You will have the mid-watch." That was twelve midnight to four in the morning. "Relieve the watch fifteen minutes before the hour. You will be the bridge talker and man the battle phone." He then showed me the sound-powered battle phone, earphones, and a button that operated the speaker which was strapped to your chest, so that it was in front of your mouth.

I went below and stowed my gear. A boatswain's mate took the new crew members on a tour of the ship. There were lots of "do's and don'ts." Three days later, 21 June 1945, I was on the bridge helping with the cleanup. Chief Quartermaster Joseph W. Kistinger called me over and told me, "We are getting underway soon, go stand in the aft corner of the bridge and keep your eyes and ears open."

The public address system announced, "Now hear this. Go to your stations all the special sea detail." The Captain and several officers came to the bridge with several enlisted men. One man had the battle phone on, so I watched him especially.

"Boiler room reports steam up."

"Engine room reports engines tested."

"All stations manned and ready Captain."

"Heave anchor to short stay."

"Anchors at short stay Captain."

"Weigh the anchor."

"Anchors aweigh Captain."

"All ahead one third."

"Steer course one six two degrees."

"All ahead two thirds."

"Set the steaming watch."

At 1416 hours, the *Albert T. Harris* was underway, on various courses and speeds, standing out of Morotai Harbor. As the ship gathered speed, I looked at the wake trailing across the blue Pacific. I had done nothing, but suddenly felt very proud. This was my ship, my shipmates, and we, along with other destroyer escorts, were charged with the guardianship of a convoy of ships transporting Australian Army personnel, vehicles, and bulk cargo on their way to Brunei Bay, Borneo.

My First Watch at Sea

Twenty-two hundred hours, or ten o'clock in the evening civilian time, was time to get some sleep. It was 21 June 1945 in the South Pacific as the public address system on the destroyer escort USS *Albert T. Harris* (DE-447) announced, "Now hear this. Lights out. The smoking lamp is out in all sleeping compartments." As the lights went out, the deck was still illuminated by the red night lights. This was to preserve your night vision—so that you could still see in the dark. Our ship was "blacked out" to avoid detection by the enemy.

At 2330 hours, the boatswain of the watch came through the racks of bunks and woke me up. I was a quartermaster striker, an apprentice, and I was to stand watch. Dressing quickly, I made my way up to the bridge of the ship. It was really dark, with the only light being the slight glimmer of starlight. I found the bridge talker and took his battle phone.

At 2345 hours, the quartermaster of the watch, Charles

Blackstone, was at my side and told me to ask all stations to re-port. "Mount fifty one manned and ready" was the first report. This was the forward five-inch gun mount manned by the gun crew and the ammunition handlers below them. The reports kept coming in from bow to stern. About one-third of the crew was on watch. Anti-aircraft, depth charges, radar, sonar, look-outs, firerooms, and engine rooms all reported in to me. Now tell the officer of the deck, "All stations manned and ready," said the quartermaster.

Our warship was underway. Our speed of advance was eight knots in patrolling station number one, three thousand yards in front of a convoy—escorting units of echelon 0-6-M—that contained LSTs (Landing Ship Tanks) loaded with Australian Army personnel, vehicles, and bulk cargo. In accordance with C.T.G. (Commander Task Group) 78.1 secret dispatch 120131 of June 1945, we were charged with protecting them on their way to Brunei Bay, Borneo.

The SU radar was sweeping the surface for enemy ships or surfaced submarines, the SA radar was sweeping the sky for enemy airplanes, and the sonar was pinging, looking for enemy submarines. The radar screen on the bridge showed the convoy behind us and the other destroyer escorts at their patrolling stations on each flank of the convoy. I was part of a team and it felt really good.

At 0045 hours, another seaman took my battle phone. Quartermaster Blackstone whispered, "Come with me. It's your turn to steer." Now I was really worried. The night sky and sea were black. How can you steer when you could not see anything?

We went to the pilothouse, where I took the wheel. In front of me was the red glow of the magnetic compass and at the side was the gyrocompass. "The course is three zero seven degrees," said the sailor that I relieved. The quartermaster explained to me that you steer by the gyrocompass but look at the magnetic compass once in a while, just to check. The trick to steering is to remember that the compass stands still and the ship turns around the compass.

I held the wheel steady to stay on the course. However the action of the wind and waves was pushing the ship slightly off course. The quartermaster showed me the lubber's line—the fixed-line display on the compass binnacle—which represents the bow of the ship. I could see that the ship was starting to go one then two degrees off course. I was instructed to turn the wheel slightly to use one or two degrees of rudder to bring the ship back on course. The compass showed the ship starting to turn. *Before* the compass showed the ship on the correct course, the quartermaster told me to turn the wheel to straighten out the rudder. The ship was back on course!

Quartermaster Blackstone explained, "There is a delay between turning the wheel and the ship's response. If you wait until the compass shows that the ship is back on course to straighten out the rudder, you will over steer. The ship's delayed reaction will cause it to continue the turn—*past* the desired course—and be off course in the other direction." I continued to steer the ship trying my best to not over steer—which takes practice.

The officer of the deck called down the voice tube, "Come left to two nine seven." I repeated back, "Left to two nine seven, sir." "Very well," replied the officer of the deck, acknowledging that I correctly understood the order. I turned the wheel counterclockwise. "It looks like the compass is turning, but in reality the compass is not moving. The ship is pivoting around the compass," explained the quartermaster, "You just steer so that the lubber's line moves towards the new course. Now put the rudder amidships. Now give her a little right rudder to stop the turn. Now report to the officer of the deck."

"Steady on course two nine seven, sir," I called out into the voice tube. "Very well," he replied. You never say, "All right." It might cause confusion.

The four hours of my first watch passed quickly, and I was soon back in my bunk. I drifted off to sleep lulled by the muted chorus of snores. I had a lot to learn, but I knew how to steer the ship!

Winding Clocks

In 1945 when I reported aboard the destroyer escort USS *Albert T. Harris* (DE-447), I was an eighteen-year-old quartermaster striker, an apprentice, assigned to the bridge gang. The chief quartermaster explained that the three chronometers on the ship had to be wound every day. It was super important to keep the precise time on these special high-grade clocks. There were three chronometers so that if one was not working correctly, the other two would display the exact same time, and you would know that the chronometer with the different time was not working properly and needed to be adjusted.

When close to land, lighthouses, church spires, towers, buoys, and other prominent points are used to determine the ship's location. When out of sight of land, the navigator can determine longitude by measuring the angle of the sun at noon, using a sextant. However accurate time was needed at dawn and dusk when the star sights were taken to determine lon-gitude *and* latitude—giving your exact location. This celestial navigation was our primary way of determining our position.

In order to test my competency for this important job, I would initially be in charge of setting and winding all twenty-three reg-ular deck clocks aboard the ship. I was to wind the clocks daily and ensure that accurate time was displayed on all deck clocks. Their locations were all over the ship, from the officers' quarters (five clocks) to the firerooms and engine rooms.

I found out that all the clocks when fully wound ran for eight days. With a little adjusting of the speed of the clocks, I was able to have an error of less than one minute after four days of running. Therefore, I had to wind and set the deck clocks only twice a week!

However, there was one deck clock that was trouble and an exception to this rule. The clock in the forward fireroom needed daily attention.

The ship's war patrol area was the South Pacific where it can get quite warm. In the fireroom, the temperature was one hundred and twenty degrees Fahrenheit. There was no air con-ditioning. The fireman and water tender on duty in this room sat directly under an air supply duct, which brought in the rela-tively cool outside air of ninety degrees on hot afternoons. Our propulsion was with steam-driven turbines.

One day, I was in the fireroom when the bridge rang up a big increase in speed. Fuel oil pipes fed the boiler and the amount of oil that was sprayed into the furnace was adjusted with dif-ferent sized nozzle tips. The fireman shut off one nozzle at a time and put on a bigger tip. When he turned the oil supply lines back on to all the nozzles, there was a big WHOOMP! The front of the boiler shuddered and right then and there I decided this was not a good place to be.

The next day I used my Boy Scout knife to unscrew the fireroom clock from the bulkhead and switched it with the one in the galley, which kept perfect time. Now I had to set the galley clock daily. I usually went just after the baker pulled the bread out of the oven. Then I helped the cooks and the baker test the bread slathered in butter.

Sometimes a bad clock can be put to a very good use.

The Head

The sanitary facilities in the United States Navy are called the "head." The origin of the term is from the days of sailing ships when the place for the crew to relieve themselves was all the way forward on either side of the bowsprit, where the *figurehead* was located. A square rigger can only sail downwind. The wind, which is moving faster than the ship, blows from the stern to the bow. The bow figurehead location was chosen because the smell was not blown onto the deck of the ship—but forward of the ship.

The crew's head on a destroyer escort was a compartment with two wide metal troughs facing each other. Flat seats were provided and seating was more or less cheek by cheek. Five sailors would sit on one side facing four sailors on the other side. A constant flow of sea water passed below the occupants for flushing.

This setup not only saved space, but provided a great conversation place. In the wardroom, the officers' conversations could not be about politics, religion, or women. The crew had no such restrictions.

One of the topics we talked about on my ship was, "What will you tell your kids that daddy did in World War II?" Today, most veterans I know will tell you that they are seldom if ever asked that question.

At certain times there would be a full house in the head because of a particularly interesting topic. "Anybody done?" would be asked by a waiting customer. If no one moved, sometimes desperate measures would be taken. A wad of toilet paper would be set on fire and floated down under the stationary bottoms, causing immediate results.

Mail Call

During the last part of World War II, I was on board a destroyer escort in the Western Pacific. To all of the crew, mail was very important. Somehow, the Navy kept the mail coming to us. When we arrived at a new anchorage, the mail was usually there awaiting us.

I liked to get mail. I found out the way to get mail was to send mail. I had a list of about twenty friends and relatives to whom I wrote.

With so many letters to write, I needed some sort of copy device. I used a hectograph, which was a flat, shallow tray, coated with a jello-like substance. I wrote my letters with a special purple ink. Smoothing the master letter on the gelatin, the ink was transferred to the surface. Then it was a simple task of putting the blank paper on top and rubbing it gently. The twentieth copy was light but readable.

Some of my shipmates did not get much mail, so I shared some of mine with them. I had one aunt who was a very good writer and her letters were always passed around the ship.

All our mail was censored. You could write only on one side of the paper so the censor could cut out the offending part. The idea was to prevent information, like troop movements, ship destinations, or equipment information, from getting to the enemy. "Loose lips sink ships" was one of the sayings.

In the Navy, on board ships, the officers censored the crew's mail and each others. My parents wanted me to keep them informed as to my location. By the time they would get my letter I would be someplace else.

I usually started my letters *"Dear Mom and Dad."* However, when the letter started *"Dear Mom & Dad & Family"* it meant this was a location letter. They were to look at the last sentence of the second paragraph. The first letter of each word, backwards, was my code.

For example, one time it read, *"I hope you get a lot of fish and of course a lot of: eels, that you especially like."*

LEYTE was spelled out! Checking the world atlas, my parents would find out that I was at Leyte Gulf in the Philippines. Mail can be so much fun!

Movies

During World War II, our ship the destroyer escort USS *Albert T. Harris* (DE-447) had a sixteen-millimeter movie projector. Hollywood movies were provided. When the ship was anchored in a safe harbor, movies were shown on the fantail (rear of the ship) each evening. The screen was on the after end of the deckhouse, with the projector alongside the five-inch gun turret.

The officers sat in the first row on chairs brought from the wardroom. The crew sat on the deck. The balcony seats were on top of the gun turret. The depth charge racks also provided good vantage points. With only one projector, there was a long pause while the next reel was wound through the twists and turns of the sound projector.

When two ships were nested together a screen was set up between the ships. Then with two projectors available, there was a continuous performance. Also, with two sources of films we often had double features.

It usually took two or three showings to give all crew members a chance to see the movie. Underway, with the ship blacked out, the movies were shown in the mess hall. Because of the smaller sized compartment, it took five or six showings for all to get a viewing. During all the movie times the ship was fully operational.

Each ship had two or possibly three movies. After they had been shown, they were traded with other ships. This only happened in port. The signalmen and quartermasters were charged with this job. Using our signal lamp, we would open and close the shutters, thereby flashing light using Morse code (dots and dashes) and visually call up other ships. We would tell the titles of our movies and ask their titles.

All movies are different. If we had a 1930's Tom Mix western and the other ship had a Betty Grable movie, there would be no deal. We were always trying to upgrade our movies and not be downgraded by the other ship. It was quite a responsibility. We never got credit for a good trade but *everyone* let us know of a bad trade.

The "Betty Grable type" movies usually had problems. By popular demand, the "good parts" were run backward and forward many times. An enjoyable bathing suit scene would be scrutinized numerous times. This would wear out and damage the film frames containing the "good parts," which ultimately had to be cut out and the remaining film spliced back together.

A Tom Mix movie's film was always in perfect condition!

Economic Lessons in Shanghai, China

In September 1945, after the peace treaty with Japan was signed, our destroyer escort the USS *Albert T. Harris* (DE-447) escorted a gaggle of amphibious ships from Okinawa, Japan, to Shanghai, China.

At Shanghai, we moored port side to starboard side of the USS *Koiner* (DE-331). We were also nested with the USS *Leslie B. Knox* (DE-580). The three nested destroy escorts were tied up to buoys—bow and stern—in the center of the Hwangpoo River off the French Bund. There were three nested British frigates ahead of us and three nested American destroyers astern. The fleet was in. The muddy Hwangpoo River was too thick to drink and too thin to plow.

Liberty started and we went ashore and exchanged our dollars for Chinese yuan. The exchange rate was 140,000 yuan for one dollar. Before the war the yuan and dollar were equal. This was runaway inflation. We mostly used 5,000 and 10,000 yuan bills.

When I got back to the ship I asked my division officer to explain to me about hyperinflation. He explained that when any government spends more than it collects, they have a deficit. In order to keep spending they borrow and/or print more paper money.

"Why do governments do this?" I asked. He explained how politicians try to give the citizens everything they want so the politicians will get re-elected.

My next question was, "What happens when a country has run-away inflation?" The answer was, "The government tries to control the inflation by causing a recession. If it isn't controlled, inflation can wipe out the middle class."

"What about the poor? Will they suffer?" I questioned. He said, "Absolutely!"

"What about the rich?" I asked. "They will pick up their wealth and leave the country," he replied.

"Why do citizens let this happen?" I wondered. "First of all, many of them are getting something for nothing from the government. Most of the rest, who eventually pay for this, do not understand what is happening and do not bother to learn what causes the runaway inflation."

I asked, "And what about the politicians?" He replied, "They propose 'feel good' legislation to make the people happy, and a little pork for the locals. Then they are home free." That was my first lesson in economics!

In China, after we left, the Communists took over the country and the rich and the middle class who did not flee the country were wiped out. The entire economy went bad. The standard of living dropped like a rock.

Only the politically connected did well.

College Wardrobe

September 1945, the war was over, the fighting done. It was time to go home. The Navy had a point system to determine who went home first. Time in service, time overseas, battle stars, commendations; the list was complex. In six months our two-hundred plus crew aboard the destroyer escort USS *Albert T. Harris* (DE-447) would be a lot less.

The older men would be going home first. They started to leave our ship when we arrived in Shanghai, China. Most transportation back home would be on any available Navy ship from aircraft carrier to cargo ships, nicknamed the "magic carpet." Only one sea bag of clothing was allowed to be taken home.

I spotted out the men leaving who were my size and in some cases bought, but mostly was given, their surplus clothing.

In February 1946, when we docked in San Francisco, California, I started shipping my newfound wardrobe home. Shortly after that I was given thirty days of leave.

It took four days by train to get back to Metuchen, New Jersey. My mother and father met me at the station. I came down the steps of the train dragging two packed sea bags behind me.

My father took one look at my cargo and said, "It's a damn good thing the Navy had that ship tied up when you left."

I went to Rutgers University thanks to the G.I. Bill of Rights. Almost all of the students were veterans and there was a predominance of Army khaki and Navy dungarees. On sixty-five dollars a month, you had to be frugal.

Japanese Battle Flags

World War II had just ended. The United States Navy destroyer escort the *Albert T. Harris* (DE-447) was steaming south off the coast of China headed for Hong Kong on a dark night. It was very strange, the ship was blacked out, radar and sonar working, the forward five-inch gun was manned and ready, depth charges ready to go just like wartime, and yet the running lights were on, just like peace time. The Navy was taking no chances.

On the ship's bridge, Quartermaster Charles Blackstone and Signalman Frank Popiel were talking. "The war is over and I don't have any souvenirs to take home," sighed Popiel.

"Why don't we make some," suggested Quartermaster Blackstone. That is how souvenir Japanese battle flags got started. The ship carried cloth to make flags. The Popiel family ran a tailor shop back home and Frank could sew. The ship had an electric sewing machine in the after steering compartment. Soon there were bunches of white flags with the red "meatball" in the middle. They were a nice size, eighteen by thirty inches. To the sailors they seemed too plain, and they would be better if they had some Japanese writing on them. A search was made of the ship but no Japanese writing was found. Finally a laundry list from a San Francisco Chinese laundry with some strange writing on it was found. Stencils were cut and soon black Chinese characters were randomly placed around the flag.

Some sailors thought the flags would look more authentic with some bullet holes and blood. The next afternoon the Captain, Commander Sidney King, gave permission for target practice on the stern of the ship. A Colt .45-caliber automatic pistol provided the holes, and sick bay provided the blood. The flags looked absolutely great.

I have wondered if one of those battle flags ever ended up in a museum, and if a Chinese couple would stare at it wondering why authentic looking Japanese characters say in Chinese "Use no starch in collar."

The Chinese Flag

During World War II, when United States Navy ships were at sea, radio silence was strictly adhered to. Pearl Harbor sent out a steady stream of coded radio messages by Morse code (dots and dashes) to all ships in the Pacific Ocean. These messages were mostly encrypted in five-letter units. All Navy ships copied down these messages every day, twenty-four hours per day. On our ship we had two radiomen on duty at all times. The ships then decoded the messages that were for their own information or action. The ships never sent back an answer, because that might give away their position to the enemy.

When ships were in sight of each other, messages were sent by International Code Flags or a flashing light blinked out a Morse code message. In port, semaphore (two flags positioned like the hands of a clock) was also used.

It was 9 October 1945 in Hong Kong Harbor. The war was over and several units of the South China Force of the United States Fleet were at anchor, including five destroyer escorts. With a crew of over two hundred men, destroyer escorts were used for convoy escort and anti-submarine and anti-aircraft support. For anti-submarine work, we had sonar, surface radar, depth charges, and hedgehogs. With air radar for aircraft detection, we had two five-inch, one quad forty-millimeter, three twin forty-millimeter, and ten twenty-millimeter anti-aircraft guns.

I was a nineteen-year-old, third class quartermaster striker aboard the destroyer escort USS *Albert T. Harris* (DE-447). My job was signal watch on the bridge of the ship.

International signal flags were run up on the flagship, the USCGC (United States Coast Guard Cutter) *Ingham* (WHEC-35). I immediately ran up the same flag hoist, at the dip (halfway up the mast). Grabbing the signal book, I looked up the meaning: STAND BY FOR ALL SHIPS MESSAGE BY SEMAPHORE. I ran our flag hoist up to the yardarm, double blocked, signaling that we understood the message.

Taking a long glass (telescope), I aimed it at the flagship. Four signalmen with flags faced the four points of the compass (so the entire fleet could see), and the message began: ON 10 OCTOBER 1945 ALL SHIPS SHALL FLY THE CHINESE NATIONAL FLAG AT THE TRUCK (masthead) AT 0800 HOURS LOCAL TIME IN HONOR OF TEN TEN DAY CHINESE INDEPENDENCE DAY. I sent the message to the officer of the deck and he called Chief Quartermaster Joseph Kistinger.

Quickly we found a picture of the Chinese National flag, obtained the fabric, and Third Class Signalman Frank Popiel went to work on our sewing machine in the after steering compartment. In a few hours we had a three-foot by five-foot flag.

The next morning, just before 0800, we gathered on the bridge. Chief Quartermaster Kistinger looked at the flag and said, "Popiel, I think it needs reinforcing on the hoist side. The wind is picking up."

Popiel went below to reinforce the flag, "But what flag do we hoist at oh eight hundred?" pondered the Chief. I volunteered that I had a small souvenir flag. "Get it," said the Chief.

At 0800, a one-foot Chinese National flag soared to the top of the mast of our 306-foot-long ship! Looking at all the other ships anchored around us, we saw only one other Chinese flag.

Soon signal lights began flashing call signs from the flagship, which sent us the following message: COMMANDING OFFICER REPORT ABOARD FLAGSHIP IMMEDIATELY.

The loudspeaker announced, "Now hear this. The crew of the motor whaleboat, man your boat." Our Captain, Commander Sidney King, quickly climbed down into the motor whaleboat. "Away the motor whaleboat, away," shouted the officer of the deck.

A few minutes later, Popiel came up with the reinforced flag and up the mast it went. The motor whaleboat soon returned. The Captain climbed up the ladder and came aboard. He looked up the mast at our reinforced three-foot by five-foot Chinese flag, took off his hat, scratched his head, and headed for the bridge. On the bridge, he told the Chief, "Admiral Buckmaster congratulated me for having one of the only two Chinese flags flying, but he asked me to make the flag four times bigger."

"Aye aye, Captain," acknowledged the Chief.

Popiel was soon back at his sewing machine with yards and yards of cloth. Several hours later we hauled up a twenty-foot-long Chinese flag, which the freshening wind displayed beautifully.

We never heard from the flagship. The moral of the story is: "If it can be misunderstood, it will be misunderstood."

A Boat Ride near Takao, Formosa

World War II was over. Our destroyer escort, the USS *Albert T. Harris* (DE-447) was leading a convoy of six LSTs (Landing Ship Tanks) and three Liberty ships from Hongay, French Indo China (Vietnam today), which was transporting elements of the 151st Division of the 62nd Chinese Army. I was a nineteen-year-old third class quartermaster.

On 22 November 1945, as we approached Takao, Formosa (Taiwan today), we met the pilot vessel LCS (Landing Craft Support) 53 and the harbor pilot, Lieutenant (junior grade) D. D. Early, came aboard. LCSs and minesweepers had spent months clearing mines from the waters around Formosa. Our ship laid to while operational orders were relayed to the vessels of the convoy. The convoy vessels unloaded the Chinese Army troops at the northern breakwater in the outer harbor, Takao.

The *Albert T. Harris* cautiously proceeded, falling in astern of LCS 53, into the harbor at Port Saie, four miles north of Takao, where there was an abandoned Japanese Naval Station. As we entered the harbor, it was littered with over two dozen sunken ships of all sizes. They had been bombed and sunk at anchor or tied up to a pier by carrier-based United States Navy airplanes during carrier raids begun in the fall of 1944. In addition, Boeing B-29 Superfortress four-engine propeller-driven heavy bombers had bombed the Takao region. Some ships had only their masts showing, while others had the whole superstructure above water.

As we slowly threaded our way through the wreckage, the

306-foot-long *Albert T. Harris*, with a thirteen-foot-four-inch draft, struck an uncharted and unidentifiable submerged object on the north side of the fifty-foot-wide channel into Port Saie, Formosa. The extent of damage was undeterminable except by a diver; however, no seams were sprung.

We moored port side to starboard side of the USCGC (United States Coast Guard Cutter) *Ingham* (WHEC-35) with Rear Admiral Elliot Buckmaster, Commander Task Group 74, South China Force, aboard. We made our port anchor chain fast to the buoy, and the *Ingham* cast off their chain from the buoy and nested with us for two days. The next day, diving operations commenced off the fantail. The port screw was found to have an eight-inch-deep chip as a result of hitting the submerged object.

In the harbor there were only two tugboats and three small speedboats left operating of a once large fleet. The tugs flew a Chinese flag but were run by the Japanese. On shore there were three two-man submarines and one one-man submarine.

The Japanese Naval Station was deserted. Almost all of the buildings were bombed, but the shops and warehouses were full. We liberated some Japanese helmets and rifles. During our two-week stay, we explored the steep hills behind the yard and found pillboxes and man-made caves all over the place. The guns and ammunition stood just as they were abandoned, except the breechblocks were missing from the guns.

One gun was still operational, and some of my crewmates had a ball firing it. They found that the ammunition could be exploded by putting it in a fire. For a while some of the fellows raised merry hell. Our Captain, Commander Sidney King, heard the gunfire and sent one of the officers ashore to make sure that *all* the breechblocks were removed and to stop the tossing of live shells into fires.

First launched in January 1943, destroyer escorts were a unique new ship specifically designed in response to the extremely successful German U-boat attacks on supply convoys between the United States and Great Britain. Designed to *escort* and protect ship convoys, these small, highly maneuverable warships were outfitted with depth charges, torpedoes and/or hedgehogs. In addition, the most sophisticated surface and air radar, plus sonar, was installed in order to search, locate, and *destroy* submarines. The *Albert T. Harris* was built with a design modified for Pacific deployment, where Japanese air attacks were more likely. One quad forty-millimeter anti-aircraft gun mount was installed amidships instead of torpedo tubes. Our ship had five-inch gun turrets fore and aft, and bristled with twenty- and forty-millimeter anti-aircraft guns.

Commissioned 29 November 1944, large contingents of the approximately two-hundred-man crew aboard the *Albert T. Harris* were enlisted teenagers of the Naval Reserve. When the war ended, the older crewmen went home first, due to the point system. Therefore, as the months passed, the average shipboard age of the shrinking crew continually decreased. Any new crewmembers were teenage boys straight out of boot camp or a Naval training school.

There was a field with twenty or more, roughly eighteen-foot-long wooden motorboats lined up. Our ship's motor mechanist removed an engine compartment cover and checked the engine. "This looks just like the engine in my 1936 Chevrolet!" he exclaimed. We soon gassed up and launched one of these boats.

One sailor sat in the small cockpit and operated the motorboat. Two other riders sat on the forward edge of the engine compartment cover with their feet dangling in the cockpit-well, behind the driver. We took turns and had a ball tearing around the sunken ships in the harbor. After finishing a turn, the motor-boat tied up alongside the *Albert T. Harris* and a new crew was put aboard. I got to go for a ride. The boat was extremely fast and you had to really hold on to not fall off. It was a lot of fun!

As the day progressed, more daring feats were performed. One group drove the boat through the bridge of a sunken Japanese cargo ship! Then a two-foot by four-foot piece of ply-wood was rigged up to a tow line. Holding a line tied to the plywood, a sailor stood on the board and as the speedboat ac-celerated, our "ski" skimmed across the surface of the water.

At the end of the day, after many wild rides, the entertain-ing boat was tied up alongside the *Albert T. Harris* for the night. Then someone unscrewed and opened the hatch at the bow of the speedboat. Inside it was loaded with TNT with a firing pin pointed forward. It was a Japanese *Shin'yō* ("Sea Quake") suicide boat!

With numerous airfields and the large pre-war Takao Naval Station, the waters around Formosa had been mined and the is-land fortified with ramparts, caves, and pillboxes, which would have been vigorously defended. Fortunately, General Douglas MacArthur had a "leapfrogging" strategy and persuaded President Franklin D. Roosevelt to invade the Philippines and by-pass Formosa. Due to their close proximity to the Philippines, Formosa's military installations were bombed and their defen-sive positions were made strategically useless. If United States troops had ever invaded Formosa, these small, fast, deadly, sui-cide boats would have attacked the Allied Fleet.

While we were speeding around all the sunken ships, if we had hit any part of those ships, our "kamikaze" speedboat prob-ably would have blown up. Some days you just have to be lucky!

❦

Garbage Mary

The destroyer escort *Albert T. Harris* (DE-447) was anchored in Hong Kong Harbor as part of the first group of American ships to arrive there at the end of World War II. The harbor was busy with Chinese sampans and junks, and a few English ships.

Aboard our ship after every meal, the galley and mess garbage cans would be emptied over the stern. Then the cans were scrubbed inside and out by the mess cooks.

Shortly after we anchored, a grubby-looking twenty-foot wooden boat sculled up alongside our quarterdeck. A poorly dressed Chinese woman asked to speak to the head cook. When the cook arrived she offered to pick up our garbage after each meal and scrub the cans. The cook accepted.

Three times a day a boat would come. The garbage cans were handed down, the garbage dumped in the boat, and the cans scrubbed. This was how "Garbage Mary" got started. Soon she was servicing every ship. The garbage was separated and sold on shore. Our garbage was better food than most people in Hong Kong had to eat.

A week later we left Hong Kong for French Indo China and Formosa. When we returned over two months later, a garbage boat approached again and offered to handle our garbage, but this was a different boat. The wood was beautifully varnished and the two-man crew wore uniforms and spoke English.

This impressive garbage boat was part of "Garbage Mary's" fleet! She had become a very rich young lady and successful businesswoman.

With the Japanese occupation over, Hong Kong became a showcase for capitalism.

Shore Patrol

The shore patrol in the Navy was usually manned by sailors from each ship in port. In order to be on the shore patrol you had to be at least a third class petty officer (that's like a sergeant).

In 1945, I was a nineteen-year-old sailor aboard a destroyer escort the USS *Albert T. Harris* (DE-447) in the Pacific. I passed all the tests and was made quartermaster third class. I spent a lot of time doing my duties on the bridge and often talked to our Captain, Commander Sidney King. I kept asking him about when I could go on shore patrol. Finally he said, "When we get back to Hong Kong you can go on shore patrol." I should point out that the Army's military police were actual policemen, all the time, and mostly protected the civilians from the military. At that time, the Navy shore patrol was the opposite; it protected the sailors from other military personnel and everyone else. The sailors you were protecting this liberty could be on the shore patrol next week protecting you.

The first day in Hong Kong our motor whaleboat took me ashore to a long pier where the shore patrol was being assembled. There were sailors from all the different ships in the harbor. I was partnered up with a chief water tender from another ship. A water tender ran the ship's boilers. He was an old man compared to the rest of us; he was in his thirties and had served in China before the war. We were issued our armbands and clubs.

Just before liberty started, and a thousand or more sailors were deposited on the pier by their boats, we were trucked to our assigned areas. In our case it was an area with lots of bars. The chief and I walked into different bars and the chief talked to the bar tenders, partly in English and partly in Chinese.

The sailors on liberty descended on the bars. Mostly they were teenagers or in their early twenties. They were not experienced drinkers and soon we had several drunks who had trouble walking. Navy trucks came through this area and we loaded the intoxicated sailors into the back of the trucks. Near the end of liberty time, the chief said we would take the next truck back to the pier because there was something there he wanted me to see.

We arrived at the long pier where boats from the ships in harbor came to pick up their men. There were timbers about six inches high running down both sides of the dock. Drunken sailors rested in various stages of collapse with their heads on the timbers. As each boat arrived, the coxswain would come onto the dock and walk past the sprawled bodies. "That one is mine, the next one is mine" would be heard as each coxswain pointed out his charges. Shore patrol assigned to the landing would help the drunks to their boats. When they arrived back at their ship, they would be undressed and washed off, if necessary, and put to bed. The United States Navy looks after their own.

On some of the cargo ships—with very high sides—a cargo net would be lowered into the boat for the disabled and sometimes passed-out drunks—who could not climb the stairway.

The sailors were piled on top of the cargo net. As the net was hauled up above the cargo ship's deck, a fresh breeze would hit the occupants, and they would be aroused. Then the yelling and cursing would start. The arms and legs sticking out of the net would start thrashing around. Imagine waking up, thirty feet up in the air with two or three other bodies in a net!

Looking back, I think my Captain set me up with the experienced chief to further my education. To this day I still do not drink alcohol.

Don't Laugh

Maneuvering a destroyer escort or any ship to tie up alongside another ship is not easy. Wind and current have to be taken into account. When pulling up alongside an oiler or ammunition resupply ship, extra caution is required so that you don't hit the moored ship, which can hold hundreds of thousands of gallons of fuel oil or live ammunition.

When docking, you want to go as slow as possible when approaching to minimize any damage if you accidently hit the other ship. The problem with this is, the slower you go, the less control you have over your ship. The wheel controls the rudders, which steer the ship. The faster the water from the propeller passes across the blade of the rudder, the more efficient it becomes. Therefore the faster you go, the more maneuverable the ship becomes. If the ship goes too slow, you lose steerageway. In addition, wind and current have more effect on a slow moving ship than on a fast moving ship. The officer at the conn (in command of the speed and direction of the ship) has to take all these factors into consideration and compromise between the maneuverability of the ship and the speed of approach. He directs the helmsman as to the compass course or the degree of rudder, left or right.

World War II had ended, and our destroyer escort, the USS *Albert T. Harris* (DE-447) was pulling up alongside an oiler for refueling in the Western Pacific. I was a nineteen-year-old helmsman at the wheel in the pilothouse and the officer of the deck was at the conn on the bridge. We slowly came alongside, and the special sea detail hurled our heaving lines over to the oiler's deck crew. A heaving line is a braided line about the diameter of a clothes line with a monkey's fist knot at the end. The size of a baseball, with a piece of lead as the middle core and looking like a bunched paw on the outside, the monkey's fist knot is tied to the end of a heaving line to serve as a weight, thereby making it easier to throw the line further. The crew on the other ship should catch the heaving line and pull the mooring line over. Our monkey's fists went flying straight out and landed with a splash in the water! We were too far away. The deck crew on the tanker started to laugh and shout at us.

Our Captain, Commander Sidney King, was on the bridge, observed this, and ordered the officer at the conn, "I'll take the conn." The Captain poked his head through the watertight door that connected to the pilothouse, three steps below, where I was still at the wheel. He ordered, "Jessen, I want you to pay extra close attention to what I tell you to do." "Aye aye, sir," I acknowledged. "Quartermaster call the engine rooms and tell them to be prompt answering the engine-order telegraph," ordered the Captain. "Aye aye, sir," acknowledged the quartermaster.

The *Albert T. Harris* got underway to make a big circle to approach the oiler again. We were "All ahead two thirds," at about ten knots. The Captain's rudder commands to me came by degrees, "Left ten degrees rudder." "Left ten degrees rudder, sir," I acknowledged. After completing the circle, we were still steaming ten knots as we headed for the oiler's side at an angle. I could see we were getting closer and closer to the oiler, and we were still "All ahead two thirds." I was *really* scared. The Captain's commands continued, "Rudder amidships." "All ahead one third." "Right five degrees rudder." "Rudder amidships." ………. "All engines stop." "Port engine back two thirds." "All stop."

The crew on the oiler saw us approaching, and they were so frightened they ran to the safety of the other side of their ship. Our fast moving, extremely maneuverable, 306-foot-long destroyer escort skidded sideways as it came alongside the oiler, quickly backed down to a stop, and gently nudged the fenders between the ships. Our crew *handed* the mooring lines to the no longer laughing crew of the oiler.

Our Captain had been a Navy flying boat pilot before taking command of our destroyer escort. You don't laugh at his ship!

Two Dollar Bills

After World War II, the Navy at Pearl Harbor, Territory of Hawaii, was reduced in size. Honolulu was still a great liberty town and thousands of sailors enjoyed it. At one point the business people started to dislike this incursion of young active men looking for some fun. They pushed the local authorities, who reacted by tightening up and enforcing laws against sailor behaviors.

Soon, in spite of Navy shore patrols, sailors were being harassed by the local police and some were arrested for acting as they always had. Apparently the business people thought the sailors would negatively influence the tourist trade.

A meeting of the commander of the naval facility and his staff was held. One plan was to restrict the sailors to the naval base. After all, the Navy had movie theaters, soda fountains, bowling alleys, and some of the best beaches.

One young officer stood up and spoke, "Sir, the answer is two dollar bills. We pay the men with two dollar bills and let them spend them in town." A heated discussion followed. How many two dollar bills would we need? How much would they weigh? Where can we get them?

It took a while, but soon a large cargo plane arrived with bales of two dollar bills. The men were paid in two dollar bills. This presented a small problem for the men as there were only two small pockets in a sailor suit.

Soon Honolulu was flooded with two dollar bills. The business community soon found out that the Navy spent a lot of money. The town started treating the sailors better.

Then the Navy paid the shipyard workers with two dollar bills just to make a point. The harassment of sailors stopped thanks to the two dollar bills.

Home from the Navy

The destroyer escort the USS *Albert T. Harris* (DE-447) returned to San Diego, California, where she was to be decommissioned. When getting discharged from the Navy after World War II, I learned that if you had a job in California, you could be discharged there instead of my original enlistment location, New York City. One of the electricians from our ship had a relative in charge of a lemon drop factory in Escondido, California, and he got a letter of employment for my shipmate Electrician's Mate Asbury Shorter (yes his last name really was Shorter) who was going to Westfield, New Jersey, and me. The Navy paid mileage back to my point of enlistment. If I took a coach across country I could save seventy-five dollars. This was a month's pay and I would get home one or two weeks sooner too.

I was discharged on 5 June 1946 at San Pedro, California. Shorter and I got on a train for the cross country trip to New Jersey. We got a cheaper rate on the train for being in uniform so we bought our tickets wearing our dress blue uniforms. The passenger cars were pulled by a coal-fired steam engine and they were very dirty. The cars were full of fine black coal soot from the steam engine smoke. As soon as we got aboard, we changed into our light blue work shirts and dungarees, and settled down for the three-and-a-half-day trip home.

Twenty paratroopers got on the train for transfer to Chicago, Illinois. They were still in the service with a top sergeant in charge. They were a real piece of work. The paratroopers were in uniform with shiny high combat boots. They were full of energy, doing pull-ups and push-ups at the drop of a hat. They even had contests doing one arm push-ups.

The sergeant asked Shorter and me what it was like to be discharged. For the first time I thought about it.

We won the war. We survived. We were going home for good. No more war. We knew about the G.I. Bill of Rights and would be able to go to college. I would have never imagined that I was wrong on two of those thoughts. I was later called up for Korea.

As the train got close to our destinations, we went into the restroom, cleaned up, and put our dress blue uniforms back on. When I arrived at the Metuchen train station, my mother and father were there to greet me at almost the exact same spot where I had left to serve in the Navy.

I remembered that two years earlier as the train approached to take me away, my mother was crying and my father tried to comfort her by saying, "We raised him and did the best we could. Now he's going off to war. He'll be tested and come back to us safe and sound and better than when he left." He was right!

CHAPTER 4

Post War

English at Rutgers

I attended Rutgers University due to the Servicemen's Readjustment Act of 1944. Commonly called the G.I. Bill, this legislation provided college or vocational education to returning World War II veterans. As a freshman in September 1946, I had to take an English test. After taking the test, I reported to the head of the English department for an interview as required.

As I sat across from the professor he rifled through a pile of papers and took out my test, which was all marked up in red pencil. He studied it briefly and then asked, "You did graduate from high school, didn't you?" I answered in the affirmative. "Your grammar needs work and your spelling is terrible. Don't you read anything?" was his next question.

"I read *The Saturday Evening Post* every week and two or three books a month," I replied, "I did get an 'A' for originality in spelling in high school."

He didn't get the joke, so I frantically tried to think of something to make amends. I said, "Sir, I don't read letters, I read words." He heard this with a grunt and told me I would hear from the English department by mail.

The mail came and I was sentenced to a spelling and remedial English class at five o'clock every weekday afternoon. I learned about the "who-whom" problem when the word was the object of a preposition—to whom.

Spelling was more of a problem. I learned "I" before "E" except after "C." Every day we had a test, twenty-five words, with ten points off for each word spelled wrong. By the third day of tests I was in the negative and owed points.

After serving my three-month sentence I was released, but some of my spelling is still very original.

The G.I. Bill

When I was discharged by the Navy after we won World War II, I attended Rutgers University. My tuition was paid for due to the Servicemen's Readjustment Act of 1944, commonly called the G.I. (Government Issue) Bill. I could receive up to five hundred dollars per year for my tuition. The tuition at Rutgers was less than five hundred dollars. So the G.I. Bill paid for my books too. I also received sixty-five dollars per month as a living allowance. I lived at home in Metuchen and took the train to school in New Brunswick, New Jersey, a nine-minute train ride. There was a Trenton Box Lunch truck on campus that sold day-old sandwiches and soda for fifty cents. This helped stretch out my sixty-five dollars per month living allowance.

Rutgers exploded with veterans and enrollment skyrocketed, mostly vets. I don't know how they accommodated all of us, but they did. I learned later that the college officials and professors were concerned at having a bunch of "killers" as students. Some of the vets were very accomplished at killing; whether hand-to-hand or with shells, bullets, or bombs.

During World War II, many enlisted men realized that they were as smart as, if not smarter than, their officers, many of whom were officers because they had gone to college. The enlisted men saw that an education can help you get ahead.

We vets were very well-behaved because we had learned discipline in the service. Also, we were older than the students of the past and we realized that future success depended upon what and how much we learned.

When the vets arrived on campus, some of the naïve upper classmen tried to get the newcomers to carry their books. They quickly realized that hazing was a bad idea.

In those days, all classes were taught by professors. The few graduate students helped out in the labs but the professors were there too. Our classes had thirty or more students but with discipline and very competent professors, it worked out well. Some of our classmates were married with children. Their lot was not easy, but they wanted an education both for themselves and their families.

Some washed out, particularly in science and engineering, but they usually transferred to another major. My time at Rutgers was not a happy time. The workload was high, and it seemed as if I was never done. When it looked as if I was catching up, more work was piled on.

The professor who taught geography had a challenge. His students had literally been all over the world. He solved this by having the students tell of their experiences, with the professor filling in the details, such as agricultural and industrial product. It was very interesting and successful.

A few students signed up for "Art Appreciation." There were not enough students for a full class, so they were shipped across New Brunswick to the New Jersey College for Women.

Soon there were tales of all the beautiful young ladies and all the dates they had. You know how young men tend to exaggerate to other young men. The next semester over a hundred Rutgers students signed up for Art Appreciation. Because of the high enrollment, the class was held at Rutgers. So much for best laid plans!

I made the special dean's list three times. This was not good. I was sent a very threatening letter each time. In Navy language, the gist of the letter was "Shape up or ship out." I shaped up and finally graduated in 1950 with a Bachelor of Science Degree in civil engineering, so I could say, "I *are* an engineer." Incidentally, my mother, Hannah Hughes Jessen, graduated in the same ceremony as me, with a degree in education!

Thermodynamics Class

Thermodynamics was one of the required engineering courses at Rutgers University. Thermodynamics is the study of energy conversion between heat and mechanical work (power). The professor who taught the class was a super smart man with many U.S. patents.

We had tests every week and a month into the course many of us were lost. About half the class, including me, flunked. Next semester we found ourselves in a "make-up" class.

Our new instructor came into the classroom and announced that he was a retired high school science teacher and he had never taught at the college level. A hushed moan went over the class. We had to pass the class and we all thought he would not be a good professor.

He started by telling of a job he had on the railroad as a fireman on a steam locomotive. He explained that a tender was located behind the locomotive with the soft coal and the water, and how he had to shovel the coal into the firebox and spread the coal around inside the firebox to keep the surface red hot. Then he spoke of the boiler above the fire with the water in a series of tubes in order to give as much surface area as possible to transfer the heat of the fire to the water. Some designs had the heat go through the tubes, thus you had either a fire tube boiler or a water tube boiler.

The water in the tubes boiled and changed to steam at a high pressure. This steam was piped down to cylinders controlled by a throttle operated by the engineer. Inside the cylinders (one on each side of the engine) were the pistons, which the steam pushed back and forth. The pistons were connected to heavy rods to turn the drive wheels. A slide valve directed the steam to alternate sides of the piston. This was called a double acting system as power was applied on both strokes of the piston.

The exhaust was directed up the stack, which caused an increase in the air draft on the fire making the coal burn faster, increasing the power. This caused the choo choo sound of the steam locomotive. The faster the steam engine went, the quicker he had to shovel the coal.

It was also his job to maintain the water level as the exhaust steam went up the stack. The exhausted steam caused the water level in the boiler to decrease so additional water had to be added.

He finished by saying, "This is thermodynamics, changing hydrocarbons into heat either by burning or exploding them and then making power. Next class we will go over the mathematics of the steam engine."

We left the class happy but wondering when we would learn something. The weekly tests came and we all passed every test.

Later on I came home and began asking my dad about gasoline engines. He answered my questions and then asked, "Why the interest?" I told him about the instructor and the steam locomotive lecture. My dad smiled and said, "Son you are lucky to have run into someone who was born to teach. It is a gift from God, like singing, that only some people have."

The Pants Tester

While attending Rutgers University on the G.I. Bill of Rights most of my classmates wore leftover clothes from World War II. Army khaki and Navy dungarees were "In."

One of my classmates supplemented his sixty-five dollar a month G.I. (Government Issue) allotment with a job as a pants tester. The pants company sent him different designs which he wore to class. He filled out a report on comments he gathered. There were different cuff designs, belt loops, and methods of preserving the crease.

Have you ever noticed how the back pocket openings on pants are horizontal while the front side pockets have a diagonal opening? The last pants the pants tester tested had the rear pockets cut on a diagonal.

Everyone thought this was great. It was easier to get things in and out and the pockets would hold a lot more.

Students were passing between classes. Many went from building to building. There was a shout, "Here comes the pants tester!" The pants tester stood at the top of a flight of stairs. He took several bows. Everyone cheered. He started down the stairs. The diagonal rear pocket caught on the end of the railing. He stumbled and tumbled down the stairs leaving a large piece of the pants hanging from the end of the railing.

The pants tester sent in his final report along with his resignation.

Now you know why rear pants pockets are the way they are and why today's building codes require the end of a staircase railing to return into the wall or newel post.

The pants tester reminded me of a poem my father taught me as a child:

> In days of old
> When knights were bold
> And sheet iron trousers they wore
> They lived in peace
> For then a crease
> Would last ten years or more

The Swarm

After World War II, I attended Rutgers University on the G.I. Bill of Rights. I lived at home, 343 Main Street, and commuted by train. One afternoon I walked up from the train and my maternal grandfather, Daniel Hughes, was waiting for me. He had never waited for me to get off the train before.

"We have a problem…there is a swarm of bees up in the middle of a tree and I can't get it," he said.

We had a couple dozen beehives in the backyard. In the spring the stronger hives would divide by swarming, usually ending up in a mass of bees on the outer branches of a tree.

We would prepare a new hive, take a pole with a basket on its end, and shake the bees into the basket. As long as you got the queen bee they would cling together and you could shake them out in front of the new hive.

I put on my long sleeve shirt, long gloves, and bee veil. Grandfather had a ladder up against the tree. I climbed up to the swarm, about twenty feet above the ground. The swarm was on a piece of limb that had been cut off. Looking up I saw where it had been cut off, about twenty feet above me. I called down, "Grandfather, what happened?"

He answered, "I climbed up and cut off the limb with the swarm, but I dropped it on the way down."

I got the limb loose and carefully carried it to the ground. I shook it in front of the new hive. The buzzing of the swarm changed tone as the queen went into the hive, followed by the rest of the bees.

I looked up at the spot grandfather had cut off the limb, forty feet up. "How could you climb up that far? You are in your late seventies, don't you have rheumatism?"

"No," he replied, "Beekeepers don't get rheumatism."

I often wonder if our scientists ever checked into that belief. For centuries it has been noted that beekeepers rarely get rheumatism, the assumption being that bee stings had a therapeutic effect. When I was a little kid we had a song:

Rheumatism, Rheumatism
How it pains, How it pains
Up and down your system
Up and down your system
When it rains, When it rains.

The Great Cannon Caper

Once upon a time, a New Jersey college possessed a cast iron cannon from the Revolutionary War. Over the years, it was stolen by a rival college several times, but always recovered.

A new college president was determined to solve this problem by planting the cannon, muzzle down, in a large lump of concrete, in front of the administration building. In fact he could see the cannon from his office window. One Monday morning he sat down at his desk to enjoy the view of the wide sweeping lawn and the cannon. He stood up and shouted, "Where is the cannon?"

Outside was a pile of dirt and a big hole in the ground. The police came and yellow crime scene tape was strung around the site. Tire marks from a heavy truck crossing the lawn were carefully measured and photographed. That afternoon a talk radio show spent an hour ranting about a college that could not protect a cast iron cannon stuck in concrete.

Reporters and cameras from two television stations showed up to interview the president of the college. He explained that he had talked to the rival college president who assured him that his college did not have the cannon. He made a public announcement that trustees were offering a ten thousand dollar reward for information on the whereabouts of the cannon.

Crowds of people started coming to look at the scene of the crime. There was a vendor at the gate selling souvenirs, a toy cannon barrel stuck in a lump of plaster.

Friday morning a large envelope was delivered to the college president, boldly marked "FOR YOUR EYES ONLY!" Inside was the front page of the rival college student newspaper. The newspaper headline read, "Look under the dirt pile." The dirt pile was moved and there was the cannon with its muzzle still stuck in the concrete. The rival student newspaper claimed the reward!

The Barber Pole

It happened in a college town. The college sat on a hill with the town below. A student came into the barber shop for a haircut. He noticed a large narrow box sitting on the floor. He asked, "What is in the box?" The barber replied, "My new outside barber pole."

"What are you going to do with your old barber pole?" asked the student. "I'll sell it to the junk man for a few bucks," replied the barber. "That pole would look great in my frat house. I will give you twenty dollars for it," came the excited offer. "Sold," was the reply. "Great! Here is the money, and my friend and I will come by this evening and remove the old pole," said the smiling student.

That evening the student and his friend unbolted the old pole and started up the street with the barber pole on their shoulders. They hadn't gotten far when a police car pulled up alongside them. The student explained the deal, but the policeman did not believe him. Soon the police car pulled into headquarters with two students sitting in the back seat and the barber pole sticking out the rear window.

The desk sergeant had heard many unusual stories before, so he decided to call the barber at home for confirmation. He released the two students and their pole. They had gotten about three blocks from the police station when a different police car pulled up alongside them. The drama was replayed.

Back in the police station, the student asked the desk sergeant to radio all the patrol cars and tell them that two students were carrying a barber pole up to the college. The radio message went out.

The next morning seven other barber poles were reported missing from town!

Patrol Craft (PC-1186)

W hile in college at Rutgers University, I served in the Naval Reserve at Perth Amboy, New Jersey. In 1946, we had a patrol craft USS PC-1186, which was a submarine chaser built during World War II. She was 175 feet long with a steel hull and usually had a complement of fifty-nine men. PC-1186 had two Hamilton diesel engines, with two shafts.

The Reservists had meetings once a week at the Naval Militia Armory on Front Street, where most of the meeting was spent educating new recruits in seamanship. In the late 1940's we took weekend trips and in July 1948 we took a training cruise to Cuba. The cruise was to be from Perth Amboy to Jacksonville, Florida, to Dry Tortuga, Florida (Fort Jefferson), and then Havana, Cuba.

When we left Perth Amboy, lots of friends and relatives were on the dock to send us off. I was a third class quartermaster at the wheel of the ship—the helmsman. The Captain was a lieutenant commander. Usually the Captain would have been an ensign or lieutenant junior grade. We had a surplus of officers on board, as this was a desirable trip.

As we left the dock by the Armory, "Cast off all lines," was the first command. Then, "All ahead one third." Our twin diesel engines rumbled into life. Then, "All stop." "All back one third." "All stop." Our Captain was trying to avoid a large anchorage area with many sailboats. "All ahead one third." "All stop." At each change of ship direction, the engines would burst into life with a cloud of black smoke.

We were about fifty feet from the dock and the tidal current was taking us backwards, past the dock. The crowd was still on the dock. The chief petty officer came up from the engine room spattered with oil and slowly wiping his hands on a rag. He spoke, "Sir, have you ever sailed on a diesel vessel?" "No chief, I've always been on steam turbines," responded the Captain.

"Well sir, let me explain something. These diesels are Hamilton diesels originally designed for powerhouses. There is no transmission. Every time you change ship direction, we have to stop the engine, and then start it up in the opposite direction using compressed air to start it. We are now out of compressed air and it will take about fifteen minutes until we get enough air to start one engine."

We had to contain ourselves from laughing as we continued to drift backwards. Finally with only the starboard engine running dead slow and a heavy right rudder, we limped away from the dock with the crowd cheering!

That was only the beginning of our trials. After several hours with both engines running, the chief came up to the Captain. "Sir, we have a problem. There are many leaks in the lubrication oil lines. We have three hundred gallons of lube oil in our tank but at this rate it won't last." A big discussion followed. One of the officers who was studying mechanical engineering went below to look at the situation.

He reported, "If we bail the oil out of the bilges and let the water settle out, we can reuse it. And we probably can stop half of the leaks." That's what we did.

The sea was rough, and then came Cape Hatteras, North Carolina. To get from the quarters aft, to the bridge area you had to cross an open deck. Waves were crashing over this area and lines were rigged fore and aft to help the crewmen get across the exposed area.

The crew's head was all the way forward at the bow of the ship. The toilet had handles on each side. With the ship pitching and rolling, you had to hang on to the handles as the toilet would drop faster than the occupant. Then on the upward pitch, you would be squished down on the seat. This certainly encouraged the bowels to move quickly!

We arrived at Jacksonville, Florida, battered but determined. We took on a deck load of lube oil in drums and filled our fuel tanks. We had lost some time with the rough weather so it was decided to skip Dry Tortuga and go directly to Cuba.

The sea calmed down, the sun was out, and all was right.

We pulled into Havana Harbor, past the Morro Castle, and tied up. Liberty would start and a line of taxicabs were ready by the dock. We had money to spend and sights to see. I bought my mother a present—a pocketbook with a baby alligator draped over the outside. It was a real alligator-skin bag and only eighteen dollars. I was proud of my bargain until months later I saw the exact same item in Perth Amboy for ten dollars.

The oil leaks were mostly fixed. The trip back was uneventful. We arrived at Perth Amboy. There was a smaller crowd on the dock and we made a perfect landing, only backing down once.

The PC-1186 only stayed in Perth Amboy for another year. There was excess corrosion on the steel hull. Some thought it was from the sulfuric acid in the water. Weak sulfuric acid attacks iron, which is the main ingredient of steel. The vessel was replaced with a wooden minesweeper.

For a training vessel, the minesweeper was probably an improvement. Torpedo-shaped devices called paravanes were fitted with a cutter and towed alongside the minesweeper. The paravanes were streamed out on each side of the ship on a long cable at about a 45 degree angle. Upon contact with the mooring cable of a mine, the jaws of the cutter cut the snared cable causing the mine to pop to the surface. The mine was then exploded by gunfire.

To set and recover paravanes takes a lot of seamanship—just what we needed for training reservists.

Don't Be a Wise Guy

Two of my summers as a college student were spent working in the Rutgers University soils lab. We were working on a graduate student's project to determine the locations of the various types of soils in New Jersey. The graduate student had worked in aerial photo interpretation during World War II. We had aerial photographs of the entire state of New Jersey taken during the winter. He had the skill to look at the photos and determine the boundaries of various types of soil.

We went out in a war surplus army truck to dig test holes at specific locations. We took three bags of dirt: top soil, just below the top soil, and three feet down. The bags were tagged and loaded into the truck.

At the lab the samples were dried and then a sieve analysis was run. A stack of sieves with different size openings was used. The soil sieves were identified by the number of wires per inch of sieve. A number ten sieve would be about an eighth-inch opening. The finest was a number two hundred sieve; that's like face powder.

Then a compaction test was run. At what moisture content can we obtain maximum density? The amount of water in soil affects its characteristics greatly; think of dust to mud. Almost everything we construct rests on soil. If the soil won't support the structure, we have to build on bedrock or pilings.

Our truck pulled up to our next location, a farmer's corn field. Our leader came back with the farmer and explained all our testing procedures and the entire project. While this was going on we dug the hole and took the samples. I was left behind to fill in the hole.

The farmer whispered to me, "What is this about?" I explained that our leader had explained it to him. He persisted, "No, what is this *really* about?" I looked around making sure everyone was back in the truck. "You're a lucky man," I said, "The government is going to build a fighter aircraft field here and you will be able to watch it all from your house."

When we returned to the soils laboratory there was a reception committee waiting for us. The professor in charge tore into me for telling a preposterous story to the farmer. One of the "suits" in the group said he was from the Governor's Office, who was also upset. It seems the farmer knew the governor. There was also a United States Air Force officer, he said nothing. I thought I would be fired or severely disciplined. But nothing happened to me for being a wise guy.

Years later I found out that an anti-aircraft missile site had been proposed for the farmer's field, but it was never built.

CHAPTER 5

Korean War

Don't Be Afraid To Ask

It was a sunny Saturday morning in November 1950 when I stepped out of the front door of my home at 343 Main Street, Metuchen, New Jersey, happily heading out to perhaps buy a used sailboat—a yawl (two masts). On the front stoop was a large envelope marked "United States Navy." I was twenty-four years of age, in the *inactive* United States Naval Reserve, and figured it was more paperwork regarding an educational course, so I walked past it. My mother, Hannah Hughes Jessen, saw the envelope and asked, "Aren't you going to open the Navy envelope before you go?" I said, "No, I'll open it when I get back." My mother said, "I think you should open that envelope, *right now!*"

I opened the envelope. A letter dated 14 November 1950 from the Department of the Navy, Bureau of Naval Personnel read: "Within 72 hours after receipt of these orders, you will proceed and report to such medical officer as may be designated in the first endorsement on the back hereof for physical examination...If found physically qualified...proceed to Yorktown, Virginia, in order to report to the Commanding Officer, Naval Schools, Mine Warfare, on 6 January 1951, for temporary active duty under instruction for a period of about thirteen weeks pending further assignment by the Bureau of Naval Personnel."

After being a sailor in World War II, I went to Rutgers University on the G.I. Bill of Rights, graduated as a civil engineer, and was working for an excavating company. I had been commissioned an ensign after completing two years of college.

I did not expect to be called back into the service, even though the Korean War was heating up.

I forgot about buying a sailboat, and instead I wrote a letter to the Navy telling them that I would be very unhappy at Naval Mine Warfare School. I respectfully requested assignment to the Naval Salvage School in Bayonne, New Jersey. I told the Navy that I really wanted to be a deep sea diver.

At the beginning of World War II, the Navy diving school was in Florida, with nice clear, warm, water. During World War II, the French ocean liner SS *Normandie* was seized by the United States authorities at New York City. In 1942, the liner caught fire while being converted to a troopship at a New York City pier. The fire department put so much water on the fire that the ship rolled over and sank on her side—with hundreds of open portholes and other openings underwater that needed to be sealed. There was a tremendous need for divers, so the Navy moved the school to New York Harbor. It was much more challenging learning to dive in the opaque waters of the Hudson River with lots of sewage in the water. After the *Normandie* was successfully raised at great expense, the restoration of the ship was deemed too costly, and she was scrapped in October 1946. The Navy diving school was moved to Bayonne, New Jersey—a better training environment.

Two weeks after I sent my letter to the Navy I received new orders: "Your orders of 14 November 1950…are hereby modified in that you will proceed to Bayonne, N. J., in order to report to the Commanding Officer, Naval School, Salvage, New York Naval Shipyard, Bayonne Annex, on 6 January 1951, for temporary active duty under instruction for a period of about fourteen weeks pending further assignment by the Bureau of Naval Personnel."

Attached to my typed orders was a handwritten note that read: "The last thing the Navy wants to do is to make you unhappy."

When I arrived at the school in January 1951, I found out that the Navy was having a difficult time finding officers who were willing to dive. I was a "live one" so they were happy to have me.

The moral of the story is: Don't be afraid to ask for something, even from the United States Navy, if you truly want it.

Dinner and a Date My Wife Never Forgot

When I received orders to rejoin the United States Navy for the Korean War, I was faced with a personal problem. Four years before, after a lot of research, I had found a very nice girlfriend—Barbara Jane Bruner. While commuting to Rutgers University, I had monopolized much of her time. She lived up the street from me in Metuchen, New Jersey, and geography was on my side. Her mother, Anna Bella Moore Bruner, was a good cook and there was pie or cake every night I called. Her mom's cherry pie was exceptional.

I knew that Naval service would be overseas, probably Korea, and that girlfriends could be lost. She was too good to be left unmarried. I met with her father, Willard Lynn Bruner, and asked if I could propose to her. His response surprised me: "It's about time." My proposal was accepted, but time was short as the Navy called. In two weeks all the arrangements were made: a church wedding, two ministers, and the reception in the large Sunday school room. My wife gets upset when I say we had to get married in a hurry, but we did.

In January 1951, I reported for duty at the United States Naval Salvage School located in Bayonne, New Jersey. I was quartered on a partially mothballed World War II escort aircraft carrier, the USS *Mission Bay* (CVE-59). Also called "Jeep carriers" because they were typically half the size of the large fleet aircraft carriers, escort carriers were slower and carried fewer airplanes and armament. Their advantage was they were less expensive and took less time to build. During World War II, escort carriers were used to escort convoys and were the center ship in hunter-killer groups which patrolled for submarines.

One weekend I was the duty officer and had to remain on the Navy base. My commanding officer suggested that I invite my wife for dinner on board the aircraft carrier and then go to the professional wrestling matches being held on the base.

My wife arrived for dinner and she was the only lady there. The other officers welcomed her and made her feel right at home, laying it on pretty thick. She enjoyed the dinner and the attention very much.

After dinner we went to the wrestling matches. We sat in the front row, almost by ourselves. The television cameras were behind us and all the sailors were on the other side of the ring so the television image would show a big audience. I was called away to the telephone.

When I returned my wife was sitting four rows back, and I asked, "What happened?"

She pointed to the ring and explained, "That man in red picked up the other man and threw him out of the ring, right alongside of me!"

As I looked where we once sat, I saw two smashed chairs as evidence confirming her story. We watched the rest of the matches from the safety of the fourth row.

Learning To Be a Deep Sea Diver

I t was January 1951 at the United States Naval Salvage School located in Bayonne, where as an ensign I began diving instruction. We were in a nice warm building that contained a large tank, ten feet deep, with portholes to observe the student divers. I sat on a platform getting dressed. Two sailors snaked me into a rubberized canvas suit. Heavy, lead-soled shoes were strapped to my feet. A heavy copper breast plate was bolted onto the suit. An eighty-pound lead belt was put around my waist, suspended from my shoulders. The copper helmet was locked on with a quarter turn. Then the air, telephone, and life lines were attached. The glass face plate was left open as an old Navy chief bent down and asked me, "How much do you weigh, sir?" I replied, "One hundred and twenty-five pounds."

With a concerned look on his face he said, "This diving suit weighs about one hundred and ninety pounds. The Navy is not going to change that. At only one hundred and twenty-five pounds ... you are not going to make it, sir." During the next six months I gained twenty pounds.

There had been a hurricane during the fall of 1950, and New York Harbor had many government ships and barges sunk or washed ashore. Salvage school began working on the real thing, which was the best way to learn. Our first diving experience was to retrieve a cargo of crates that had been swept off a barge during the storm. Because of the cold water we had three-finger gloves attached to our diving suit. After getting dressed in the diving gear, the face plate was bolted closed. A diver's tender on each side of me helped me over to the ladder where I climbed down into the water. I opened the air valve and slid down the descending line. When my feet reached the bottom, I adjusted the air valve until the water pressure squeezed me up to my chest.

The water in New York Harbor was cold, but warmer than the air temperature, and it was so dirty that you could not see your hand in front of your face. Bayonne is located in New Jersey directly across the Hudson River from New York City. There was raw sewage, including human waste, dumped from New York City floating in the water. I could not see much of anything being thirty feet underwater, and, with my three-finger gloves, I could feel very little; but I had to find the sunken crates. Feeling around I found one and took the hoist line and began fastening it to the crate. After tying the knots fastening the hoist line to the three-foot-cubed crate, I told the divers topside to haul it up.

I was soon working on my third crate, but for some reason this crate was giving me a lot of trouble. It was very difficult to get a line attached to it, and after several minutes of trying, a voice came over the telephone, "Mr. Jessen let go of the last crate. You are tying up the other diver!"

While I was busy working, a second diver had hit the bottom. Before he could find any crates, he thought he was being attacked by a giant sea monster. He screamed bloody murder to the diver's tenders topside. After reaching the surface we had a good laugh, and I apologized for mistaking him for a crate.

Celestial Navigation at Sea

I was assigned to serve as an officer aboard the rescue salvage ship the USS *Conserver* (ARS-39) stationed in the Pacific in May 1951. Rescue salvage ships are designed for rendering assistance to disabled ships, salvage, diving, towing, firefighting, and heavy lifting.

One of my duties as a lieutenant junior grade was navigator. On small ships the navigator stood the 0400 to 0800 watch in the mornings and the 1600 to 2000 watch in the evenings. This was because in order to navigate, you had to measure the angles between certain stars and the horizon. You had to be able to see the horizon and the stars at the same time.

Before sunrise we would examine the sky and locate the stars we would use. Every navigator had their favorite stars. There is Orion; his belt is easy to pick out, marching across the sky with Sirius (the Dog Star) right behind. The Big Dipper, part of the constellation Ursa Major (the Great Bear) was there, but the North Star was dim and took more skill to get a good sight.

At the right time, the quartermaster would bring out the

sextant, hand it to the navigator, and take out the stop watch he had set from the ship's chronometers. Taking the sights could take ten to twenty minutes. When the ship was pitching and rolling, the skill factor came in. After the sights were taken, the navigator would consult a series of tables to get the results.

This is how a ship's location is determined in the middle of the ocean. Each sight on a star produces a line of position at right angles to the bearing of the star. At that exact time and angle, there is an imaginary upside down cone circling the surface of the earth and the ship is somewhere on that imaginary line. You get one line of position from each star. Therefore you need to get several star sightings to try to get the imaginary lines to intersect to determine your position.

I liked to get six or eight sights, more if it was rough. These were then plotted, moving each one ahead to the last sight. At fifteen knots, we would have traveled five nautical miles in twenty minutes. Hopefully the lines would all cross in one spot. If the plotted lines were within a mile or two, you would pick a spot.

When you could not see the stars due to rain or clouds, navigation was by dead reckoning. The navigator would plot the course being steered and the speed on the chart. If you were in a storm, you would not know the exact course and speed "made good" because of the effect of the wind and waves upon the ship. If a storm had lasted three days, you would have traveled over a thousand nautical miles. That is when dead reckoning gets tough. The actual ship location could be hundreds of nautical miles away from the dead reckoning location. That makes you worry.

Today with GPS (global positioning system) finding your ship's location is easy. I hope the Navy still uses the stars. When the bad guys attack the United States in the next big war, the first thing they will do is knock out the satellites. There is a lot of skill required in celestial navigation and sailors need to be prepared.

Buoys at Kwajalein

In July 1951, I was the diving and salvage officer aboard the rescue salvage ship the USS *Conserver* (ARS-39). We were at Kwajalein, an atoll in the Marshall Islands, to lay mooring buoys for battleships and aircraft carriers.

The island was hot and the sun's reflection off the white coral hurt your eyes. The trees had been cut down by shell fire from the Battle of Kwajalein during World War II and were still just short new trees or stumps. Japanese guns from World War II were placed about the island as monuments and there were battered pillboxes here and there. Everything was run-down and rusty.

The mooring buoy system consisted of a buoy connected to a six foot cube of concrete with three anchors stretched out 120 degrees apart. The anchors were attached to the cube with 2½-inch chains. Each link of the chain was a 2½-inch diameter bar bent in an ellipse. The challenge was to stretch out all these chains tightly.

On a previous job of laying mooring buoys, that ship's crew had worked everything from their rescue salvage ship. They had beaten up their ship's sides severely with the heavy weights. We wanted a plan that would avoid damaging our ship.

While attending the United States Naval Salvage School in Bayonne, New Jersey, I gained practical experience in pulling government vessels—that had been driven aground in a hurricane—off the shoreline. The salvage equipment had been set up on a large barge and moved from site to site.

During the trip from Pearl Harbor, Territory of Hawaii, to Kwajalein, there were in-depth discussions as to different plans. It was decided to try to work off a barge, if we could get a barge, and, if possible, use a crane to handle the heavy weights. Otherwise, we would have to use the booms on our ship.

When we got to Kwajalein, there was a large barge available. The United States Air Force inadvertently supplied a crane. I suggested to the Captain that we paint the crane a different color, but he wouldn't agree. Nonetheless, it took the Air Force a week before they missed it! There was also a small tugboat assigned to us.

We hung the large anchors over the sides of the barge attached with pelican hooks—hinged hooks that we could quickly release by a sliding ring. The heavy chains were attached and draped over the side of the barge in twenty-foot bights, held in place with manila lines tied to cleats we installed. The concrete cube was on the barge deck. The riser chain to the buoy was attached to the concrete cube at one end and tied at the other end to a ½-inch steel cable, which was attached to an oil drum that was being used as a float.

The small tug handled the barge. The locations were marked with marker buoys. The first anchor was dropped and the chain was payed out by breaking the manila line, sometimes helped by an axe. Then the concrete cube with the riser chain, steel cable, and oil drum attached, was dropped. Next the second anchor was dropped, stretching out the second chain. Then the third anchor was tugged to its location, dragging the chain along the bottom. Later the mooring buoy was attached to the riser chain from the concrete cube.

Sometimes there are problems. One of the oil drum floats attached to the steel cable, which was attached to the riser chain, had sunk. It was probably hit by a passing ship at night. We would have to dive to retrieve the steel cable.

On 17 July 1951, it was my turn to dive. Divers get paid extra for the time they spend underwater diving, so everyone takes turns. We were diving off a small barge with a crane called the *Mary Ann*. I was shaken down into a heavy rubberized canvas suit. The Pacific Ocean was warm, so my hands went through rubber wrist cuffs (if the water was cold, three-finger gloves would have been fastened to the arms of the suit). The heavy copper breast plate was fitted over my shoulders and firmly bolted to the suit. Heavy lead-soled shoes were fastened to my feet. The copper diving helmet was put on and locked with a quarter turn. The eighty-pound lead belt was secured with straps over my shoulders. The air, telephone, and life lines were attached. The face plate was bolted closed. I tested my air and telephone.

With a diver's tender at each side, I walked to the stage. This was a platform raised and lowered by a crane. Standing on the stage with legs astride, I was lowered into the water. What a relief! The weight of the diving rig disappeared from my shoulders. I opened my air valve a little and signaled to be hauled by the lifeline over to the descending line.

I grabbed the descending line and started to slide down, opening my air valve as the water pressure increased. Divers descend as fast as they can because the limited time you can stay on the bottom starts as soon as you leave the surface.

On the *Mary Ann*, one diver's tender "tended" my lifeline, air hose, and telephone line by keeping a slight tension so the lines stayed above me as I moved around the bottom. The other tender watched the air compressor and listened to the telephone, answering any calls.

The water was clear. As I approached the bottom, I spotted an anchor chain. "On the bottom," I reported to the surface using the telephone. I adjusted my air valve so the pressure came just to my chest. Leaning forward, I slowly walked to the chain, my lead-soled shoes kicking up a little silt. I followed the chain until I came to the end, there was the anchor! Wrong end, so I walked the other way. I found the concrete cube and there was the riser chain in a pile with the sunken oil drum nearby. Then back to the descending line which I moved to the concrete cube for the next diver.

My time on the bottom was up.

I was hauled up by the lifeline to one hundred feet of depth. I hung there moving my arms and legs, beginning to get the excess nitrogen out of my body.

The decompression time was set by tables reflecting the depth (one hundred and eighty feet) and the time on the bottom. At the next stop, I was met by the stage, which I climbed back on and stood legs astride. The stage let you exercise easier.

All of this exercise and waiting time at various depths was done to prevent decompression sickness. Called "the bends" or Caisson disease, decompression sickness is a dangerous, extremely painful, and occasionally lethal condition caused by nitrogen bubbles that form in the blood and other tissue when a diver is brought to the surface too quickly.

The time I reached the surface was documented in the ship's log book, in addition to the time I left the surface. The total elapsed dive time was ninety-two minutes.

The next diver went down and attached a line to the steel cable and the damaged oil drum. Our diving job was done. Later the riser chain was attached to the floating buoy.

After diving in the polluted Hudson River, diving in the clear Pacific Ocean was a piece of cake!

Tattoos

Tattoos used to be a Navy thing. We had one sailor who had his girlfriend's name "Sally" tattooed on his chest with a heart and a cupid. Sally was not impressed; she thought it was gross and she left him. After that, every time he went to a U.S.O. (United Service Organization) dance he always looked for another Sally. I often wonder if he ever found her. If he did, I hope she was kind to him.

Another old salt would approach you and ask, "Do you want to see my crabs?" If you said, "Yes," he would turn around, pull up his pant legs, and show you a Jersey blue crab tattooed on each calf.

A boatswain's mate had just transferred aboard the rescue salvage ship the USS *Conserver* (ARS-39) during the Korean War. He had a truly remarkable tattoo on his chest. It was a standing naked lady, rendered in exquisite detail. He was working on the forward deck without a shirt. The Captain, Lieutenant William McGee, shouted at him and called him up to the bridge.

"How long have you had that?" asked the Captain pointing at the tattoo.

"Over a year, sir" was the reply, "Isn't it great? It's a copy of a 'Petty Girl' from a men's magazine, sir."

"When we get back to Pearl Harbor, you get a swimsuit tattooed on it," order the Captain. The Bosun pleaded with Captain McGee, but the Captain would not budge.

Weeks later we returned to Pearl Harbor. We were tied up at the "Able" dock for two weeks. The Captain figured that the Bosun had had ample time to get the swimsuit tattooed.

At the next weekly inspection, the Captain stopped in front of the Bosun and ordered him to raise his jumper and skivvy shirt. The jumper and skivvy shirt were slowly raised and there was the tattooed lady wearing a white swimsuit cut out of adhesive tape!

Captain McGee broke into a laugh. Then the whole crew started to laugh. "OK, I give up," said the Captain, "But I want that white swimsuit on for every inspection." The crew had a contest to name the lady—Sally won.

At subsequent inspections the white adhesive tape bathing suit was replaced with various colored dresses. At one inspection Sally the tattoo wore slacks! We all looked forward to seeing the "Petty Girl" wearing the latest fashions.

The Decimal Point

As United States Navy hard hat divers during the Korean War, we were dressed in a copper helmet, a rubberized canvas suit, heavy lead-soled shoes, and an eighty-pound lead belt around the waist. The helmet and suit (rig) were filled up with compressed air. This air was used for breathing and to control the movement of the diver.

A hard hat diver adjusts his air valve to control the squeeze of the water pressure from his chest down. If he has to pick something up from the bottom, he leans his head forward and pushes a button inside the helmet with his chin. This is called the chin button, and it increases the amount of air exhausted from the rig. The buoyancy is reduced, and he slowly drifts down toward the bottom—his body straight but leaning forward. After the diver picks up the object, he grabs the chin button with his mouth, pulls it, and this closes the valve. The rig increases the buoyancy by filling with more air and he regains his standing position.

Now, you have to understand the diving helmet, in order to understand the problem. You are not supposed to dive if you have a cold or head congestion. This can cause severe pain in the ears. To prevent the spread of infection, the helmets were to be swabbed out with grain alcohol to sanitize them.

Grain alcohol is drinkable and very desirable, so it was kept locked up in the diving locker. There was also grain alcohol in the magnetic compasses, which were liquid compasses located on top of the binnacle on the bridge and in the after steering compartment. Because it would not freeze, grain alcohol was used to float the magnetic compass card so it would not have excessive swing or wobble, as the ship pitched and rolled through the waves. There have been incidents in the Navy where a ship's operational assignment was in a warm area and when the ship moved to an area with below freezing temperatures, the compass liquid froze and the glass broke, because someone had drained the grain alcohol out of the compass and replaced it with water!

We used three to four quarts of grain alcohol every three months depending on the diving requirements. As the diving officer, I typed a requisition for four (4.0) one-quart cans of grain alcohol. *Somehow,* the decimal point slid over and the requisition was for forty (40.0) one-quart cans. The requisition was signed by the proper authority—one of many requisitions—and sent in.

A month later, forty one-quart cans of grain alcohol arrived. Four cans went to the diving locker where they were locked up. The balance went to my cabin—trading goods.

I was amazed at my good fortune! The rescue salvage ship the USS *Conserver* (ARS-39) was moored at Berth "Sail 16," U.S. Naval Submarine Base, Pearl Harbor, Territory of Hawaii, for repairs. Among the many things in need of shipyard attention were the main engines and the guns. This was during the Korean War and there was a budget with only enough money for the engine repairs.

I learned that grain alcohol not only sanitized our diving helmets, but also had a remarkable ability to get our two twin forty-millimeter guns repaired. Ten quarts of grain alcohol and one hundred pounds of coffee did the job. Our anti-aircraft guns were now operational *and* the battered wardroom chairs suddenly were replaced with new chairs, just for good measure.

After I left the ship, I wondered if the 40.0 one-quart cans of grain alcohol arrived every three months. If they did, I hope they were spent wisely.

Passing Inspection

During the Korean War, I was assigned to the 213-foot-6-inch-long rescue salvage ship, the USS *Conserver* (ARS-39), which had a crew of eighty men. Among my many duties, I was the gunnery officer. Our main armament was two twin forty-millimeter guns and four twenty-millimeter guns. We were at Pearl Harbor getting ready to relieve another ship already at Korea. I had three gunner's mates working with me and we worked very hard to get the guns in shape; they needed a lot of work.

Every Saturday was the Captain's inspection, and he always found something wrong with our guns. I was determined that we would do everything perfectly and we would pass inspection with flying colors.

The day that we worked so hard for finally arrived, and the Captain, Lieutenant William McGee, could not find anything wrong, so he ordered, "Paint the guns."

I was crestfallen at our guns being rejected again. As I sat on the stern of the ship where I was feeling sorry for myself, a chief petty officer walked up to me and asked, "Mr. Jessen, what's the trouble, sir?"

I told him of my try for perfection and how I could not make the Captain happy because he could always say, "Paint it." He thought for awhile and said, "Sir, the Captain is a nut on grease fittings. He always wants them shinny with just a dab of grease, with no paint on them, and no rust."

I replied, "I know all that. I personally check them all out before every inspection."

"Let me give you a little advice, sir," said the chief in a calm soothing voice. "Get yourself a dozen grease fittings. Get some that are rusty, put paint on other ones, and remove the grease from some other ones. Then have the gunner's mate replace the perfect ones with these. Make sure you spread them around because all your guns must have a hundred fittings on them. This allows the Captain to find something wrong that will be easy to fix."

That is exactly what we did. Captain McGee was happy; he usually found about half of them. We were happy because it became like a game for us to see how many the Captain could find.

But I learned an important lesson. When having inspections, always have something wrong that is easy to find, and easy to fix. Otherwise they will find something that is hard to fix or a lot of work.

How to Get Supplies for Your Ship

One of the jobs of a rescue salvage ship is to get stranded vessels off the beach, or, to be exact, to help the stranded vessel to get itself off the beach. To do this, the salvage ship goes in close to the stranded vessel and fires a thin nylon line to the crew with a line throwing gun. This enables them to pull in a manila line and then a ½-inch steel cable. This is attached to a 1⅝-inch cable that is fastened to the stranded vessel. Then the salvage ship stretches the cable.

The other end of the 1⅝-inch cable is attached to ninety feet of battleship anchor chain ending with a 15,000-pound anchor, which the salvage ship drops to the bottom. This "beach gear" is tightened by the stranded vessel with a large block and tackle using a seven-ton winch that eventually puts a fifty-ton strain on the cable. To attach the pulling force requires a connector (called a carpenter stopper) to the 1⅝-inch cable. Each set of beach gear required two carpenter stoppers—one to pull with, and the other to hold the 1⅝-inch cable while the block and tackle were stretched out for the next pull.

Now to the story…

During the Korean War, when I got on board our rescue salvage ship the USS *Conserver* (ARS-39) we were short four carpenter stoppers. I was told, "Not to worry because a requisition had been submitted and we are covered." A requisition form is sent to the supply department, and, if approved, the supplies should arrive. If you are missing an important item from your ship and you are inspected, you will not fail the inspection if you provide a requisition showing that you have requested the item. That was why we were "covered." Our ship was leaving shortly for Korea and I knew I could not hold a fifty-ton strain with a paper requisition!

At the U.S. Naval Base at Pearl Harbor in the Territory of Hawaii, I checked with the warehouse where the carpenter stoppers were stored. The requisition had not arrived, but I was told, "Don't worry, you are covered."

The next day I went to the motor pool and took out a truck. With an eight-man working party, we went to the warehouse just before lunchtime.

We parked the truck in the doorway of the warehouse so they could not close and lock the doors. When asked to move the truck I said, "Our driver with the keys went to lunch." When the coast was clear—all the warehouse personnel had gone to lunch—we went inside the warehouse to the location of the carpenter stoppers. They were heavy and packed in substantial wooden boxes. We carefully opened the boxes, removed the stoppers, replaced them with concrete bricks, and resealed the boxes. Then we hurried back to the ship.

The next morning at 0913 we were underway from Berth "Able 12," Bishops Point, with a harbor tug the USS *Osceola* (YTB-129) in tow, enroute to Eniwetok in the Marshall Islands.

The many months while I was on board ship, the requisitioned carpenter stoppers never arrived. I was hoping *we* would receive the boxes of concrete bricks. I wondered what would happen when the boxes of concrete bricks got delivered to some other ship. Or perhaps they are still in the warehouse at Pearl Harbor!

Midnight Requisitions

I n August 1951, I was the diving and salvage officer on the rescue salvage ship the USS *Conserver* (ARS-39) as it entered the harbor at Eniwetok Atoll in the Marshall Islands. We had just come from Pearl Harbor where most of our requisitions for spare parts and supplies had not been filled. The United States Navy was short on money and supplies since most materials went to Europe where our intelligence thought the real war would occur.

Our "Korean Police Action" was a very low priority war. We found out Eniwetok was the supply base for the atomic tests at Bikini Atoll. The Atomic Energy Commission's warehouses were filled with things we needed and were lightly guarded.

As we went about our job of underwater repair work to a pipeline, some of our crew went on a reconnaissance mission and located the supplies we needed. Every night our workboat made clandestine trips to the shore. The Captain, Lieutenant William McGee, and the Executive Officer, Lieutenant A. R. Davis, did not know of this operation, as it was mostly my salvage crew that did the "requisition" of the supplies we needed.

In the middle of the night our workboat had returned from the beach. Out of habit, the coxswain rang the bell twice to tell the engineer to stop the engine. He was not supposed to ring the bell in this secret circumstance.

The ding-ding sound of the bell woke up the executive officer. He came to the stern of the ship where the workboat was being unloaded. "What are you men doing?" he shouted.

"Unloading paint, sir," was the response. Over one hundred one-gallon cans of paint were stacked on the deck with more in the workboat.

"Where did you get all that paint?" asked the executive officer.

"Found it on the beach, sir," the sailor responded.

"What do you mean you found it? You guys stole it, didn't you?" questioned the now excited and worried officer.

"I guess you could say that, sir. But they have lots of stuff there and it all belongs to the government," was the reply.

"*Take it all back!*" ordered the exec. The paint cans started to be loaded back into the workboat.

The sailor looked up at the executive officer and asked, "Mr. Davis, what do I tell them if we get caught putting all the paint back, sir?"

The exec scratched his chin and thought for a moment and then said, "OK bring it aboard. But tell me, why so much paint? It will take years for us to use it all up."

The sailor got a big smile as he answered, "It's for trading stuff, sir. We couldn't find any toilet paper!"

The Officer's Hat

In Sasabo, Japan, during the Korean War, our ship was asked to send a shallow water diver to put temporary plugs in some water inlets of a very large U.S. Navy cargo ship, the USS *Castor* (AS-1). This was before scuba diving and our gear consisted of a face mask, weight belt, and attached lifeline and air hose. Two men and I went to the ship. The ship's chief engineer had marked the locations of the holes to be plugged and the depth. The ship was loaded with cargo, so the holes were twenty to twenty-five feet underwater.

We set up our air compressor and rigged a ladder over the face of the dock. I was the diving officer but I took my turn with the rest of the divers. It was my turn to dive and the water was warm, so instead of the usual rubberized suit, we used two layers of diving underwear that had long sleeves and long legs. This was protection against the sharp marine growth (barnacles) on the dock.

I stripped down, put on the underwear, belt, and mask, picked up the wooden plugs and a hammer, and entered the water. I found the holes and hammered the plugs in. A line was attached to each plug so they could be pulled out later.

I climbed back up on the dock and stripped off my gear. We had forgotten a towel so I was air drying.

Next thing I knew, a jeep pulled up to the dock, and four USO (United Service Organizations) ladies got out. My head diver yelled loudly, "Quick Mr. Jessen, put on your hat, so they know you are an officer, sir!"

Thinking quickly, I dove off the dock back into the water. The chief engineer saw all of this from the cargo ship's deck above.

After he finished laughing, he sent down a towel for me.

LST on the Rocks

The United States Navy LST (Landing Ship Tank) from World War II was 328 feet long and could carry 2,100 tons of cargo. It landed bow first onto the beach, opened up its doors, and lowered a ramp. The cargo it carried, usually tanks, trucks, or jeeps, went directly ashore, without the need of any port facilities.

During the Korean War, the United States Navy was short of sailors and many World War II veterans like myself got called back to help. There were still not enough crews to man all the ships, so a Japanese company SCAJAP (Shipping Control Authority for the Japanese Merchant Marine) was used that operated United States Navy ships (such as an LST) with crews of Imperial Japanese Navy veterans of World War II. SCAJAP was originally established after World War II for the repatriation of Japanese war personnel.

One of these Japanese operated LSTs, Q019, was flooding (taking on water) near the town of Chikura, off the coast of Japan. The skipper beached her on Kottono Hana Point; however, he missed the sandy beach and put the LST up on the only rocks for miles in each direction, broadside to the beach. A Japanese salvage company had tried to get the ship afloat but failed.

The Captain, Lieutenant William McGee, of our rescue salvage ship the USS *Conserver* (ARS-39) was at the officers' club and heard about the troublesome LST. He bragged that his crew could get her afloat. Subsequently we received orders to salvage the LST.

When I got aboard the stricken vessel as the salvage officer, the Japanese salvage party was still aboard and you could see why they had failed. The main engine room was flooded, and this would be a major challenge that needed some Yankee ingenuity.

This salvage was a very complicated task, so I had drawn a diagram of my design on the bulkhead of the LST, in order to explain the plan of attack to my crew. To pull the ship off the beach we set four 15,000-pound anchors with hundreds of feet of 1⅝-inch cable. We used the four carpenter stoppers we had "requisitioned" from the warehouse at Pearl Harbor. To lighten the ship, we sealed the engine room and set up air compressors to force air into the sealed compartment—forcing out most of the water.

This was very difficult and hard work that we finished. We were just about ready to pull the ship off the beach, when a helicopter landed on the shore and a full United States Navy Commander was ferried out to inspect our progress. When he came aboard I was down in the bilge pouring concrete over some temporary patches. I was sent for and arrived on deck spattered with concrete, dirt, and oil stains. I had not changed my clothes or taken a shower in three days. I had a certain unique air about me.

The Commander asked me to explain our plan to get the ship afloat again. I showed him the diagram I had drawn on the bulkhead and explained it to him. He then started suggesting changes, like move this anchor a little this way, others that way. My mind was racing, thinking about what to say, as he was adding another two or three days of unnecessary work to the salvage.

I said, "Commander your plan sounds much better than mine. Just so I get everything right, would you mind putting that in writing for me, sir?"

The Commander looked me over, then looked at the deck of the LST scattered with pumps, air compressors, tackles, winches, and cables everywhere. He patted me on the back and said, "Lieutenant you are doing just fine."

We continued to work on the Q019 and successfully pulled the LST off the rocks and got her afloat again.

Mission accomplished!

The Lost Library

The "Korean Police Action" was a war on a budget. As an example, the trucks used to haul provisions and supplies were leftovers from World War II. At the end of the war, as United States forces were withdrawn from the islands and jungles, most of the equipment was abandoned. When the Korean War started, a lot of this equipment was brought to Japan, repaired, rejuvenated, and sent to Korea. Most ten-wheel trucks in Korea did not have tires for all of the wheels!

The new trucks and equipment went to Germany. Our high command thought that was where the fighting would be. Maybe the Russians didn't attack Europe because they knew we had the new trucks there, and the Chinese attacked in Korea because they knew we had the old trucks without enough tires there.

On our rescue salvage ship the USS *Conserver* (ARS-39) we could not get winter crankcase oil in the very cold winter. We had to drain the heavy summer oil, heat it almost to a boil, and quickly pour it into the engine to get it started!

However, the most serious supply problem happened during the several weeks we spent salvaging the SCAJAP LST (Landing Ship Tank) Q019 near Chikura, off the coast of Japan. The crew was really down in the dumps. No mail, no liberty, and on 27 November 1951, no toilet paper! I was the morale officer and knew this was a major problem needing immediate action.

The first toilet paper replacement resource was the ship's

library. It was strange to see someone in the head reading a book and then tearing out a few pages as a toilet paper substitute. We were still on the salvage job when the library expired. Next, it was official correspondence that was used. Symbolically the first to go were copies of the requisitions for toilet paper!

The official correspondence was information carbon copied on onionskin paper. Onionskin is a thin, canary colored, lightweight, strong, translucent paper used with carbon paper for typing duplicates on a typewriter. All the carbon did not stay on the onionskin paper when used. I was also the medical officer and determined that bluish bottoms were not a health concern.

On 5 December 1951, we finished towing Q019 to the dry dock and anchored off the United States Naval Base at Yokosuka, Japan, where there were supplies being unloaded. I sent my best "cumshaw artist" ashore with twenty pounds of coffee and six #10 cans of ketchup for trading. Cumshaw artist is a Naval term for one who is adept at getting projects done by "obtaining" items for free, or bartering for needed material and/or services.

My definition of a cumshaw artist is someone you send out to get you something, and when they come back, you don't ask them where they got it!

When our workboat returned, my cumshaw artist had four cases of toilet paper. The crew manning the rail greeted him with a rousing cheer. He also brought the coffee back!

The Jeep Ride

W hile working as the diving and salvage officer aboard the rescue salvage ship the USS *Conserver* (ARS-39) the divers would often tell me stories. Here's one...

During World War II an officers' club was on top of a small hill on a Pacific island. The road leaving the club went straight down to the shore, then on to a floating dock. Just before the dock, another road swung left to the Seabee (CB, Construction Battalion) base.

Ensign Benson* finished a great evening by having lots to drink while he listened as his CO (commanding officer) told sea stories. "Take my jeep back to the Seabee base," ordered his CO, "I'll catch a ride with Roberts*."

Ensign Benson started off down the hill. He was a little woozy. He missed the turn and drove the jeep right off the end of the dock!

Soon a very wet ensign appeared at the officers' club to report the mishap to the CO. A very understanding CO replied, "Don't worry. There is a salvage ship out in the harbor. Tomorrow we will borrow a diver and get the jeep back."

The next morning a hard hat diver was getting dressed at the end of the dock. An air compressor was thumping away building up pressure. Soon a crowd began gathering.

Ensign Benson watched anxiously as an eighty-pound lead belt was buckled around the diver. With diver's tenders at his side, the diver rose and was helped over to the temporary ladder, which he began to climb down. He slipped into the fifty-foot-deep water.

Everyone watched the water as the bubbles from the diver moved back and forth. After about twenty minutes of walking around the bottom of the bay, the diver signaled to be hauled up. The diver's tenders heaved on the lifeline and soon the diver was sitting on the bench. His copper helmet was removed.

Ensign Benson anxiously asked, "Did you find it?"

"What is the number on the jeep, sir?" asked the diver.

"Why do you need to know that?" questioned Ensign Benson.

The diver answered, "Because there are five jeeps down there, sir. That's why!"

*Fictitious name.

My First Cup of Coffee

Two years in the Navy, four years of college, and I still did not drink coffee. Pepsi-Cola was my drink.

It was winter in late 1951 and our rescue salvage ship the USS *Conserver* (ARS-39) was off the east coast of Korea at Chumonshin, just south of the 38th Parallel. The sea was rough. The Captain, Lieutenant William McGee, ordered me to take our motor whaleboat into the small harbor to inspect an LST (Landing Ship Tank). This port was used to bring in supplies, including drums of jet fuel. Korean laborers were used to unload the ships.

The motor whaleboat was a very good sea boat because it was double-ended with a pointed bow and stern. After an exciting launch we started in. The waves were big and we climbed up each wave and then shot down the back of the wave. The spray flew over the gunnels and we were soon covered with ice.

We pulled in behind the harbor breakwater and tied up. I was looking for a Marine sergeant in charge of unloading the LSTs. Two ships were pulled up to the beach, the bow doors were open and the ramps were down. A swarm of Korean laborers—small, squat, very strong men—were loading U.S. Army trucks with drums of jet fuel.

I spotted a pyramid tent with smoke pouring out of the stack in the rear. Walking into the tent with ice still stuck to my coat, Marine Corps Sergeant Seegler greeted me with a snappy salute. Then he thrust a cup of hot coffee into my hand.

"I don't drink coffee," I said.

"You do now, sir," he replied and he was right.

After a second cup, we visited the LST with the problem. A one-inch steel kedging cable was wrapped around its screw. We could fix that, and we did.

The Sergeant showed me around his operation. At one end of the beach was a huge pile of empty fifty-five-gallon drums, neatly stacked. "What's that all about?" I asked.

"Bungs, sir," he said, "We can't send back empty drums unless they have a bung in each one. They lose the stoppers up at the airfield, so the drums cannot be shipped back."

"I requested fifteen hundred bungs two months ago," he continued, "and the supply officer shot back a letter asking why I needed fifteen hundred bungs. I answered the officer explaining my pile of empty drums, but I probably never will get them. So the drums will just continue to be piled up."

I learned on this trip about government inefficiency and how to drink coffee.

The Dropped Boat

During the Korean War on 14 February 1952, I was transferred from the rescue salvage ship the USS *Conserver* (ARS-39) to the USS *Current* (ARS-22). The *Current* had just been taken out of "mothballs" and been re-activated. She had a new pickup crew. I was transferred to the *Current* to be their diving and salvage officer. I had attended Naval Salvage School in Bayonne, New Jersey, at the same time as Lieutenant Charles Tiernan, the *Current's* Captain, and I knew him. We were moored to a buoy in the harbor at Sasebo, Japan, and the *Current* was to tie up alongside. I had my gear packed and watched as the *Current* came in to our port side. She hove to a few hundred feet away from us and started to lower a workboat that was on the same side that would be tied up to us.

As the davits swung the workboat over the water, suddenly the stern of the boat dropped and the three-man crew tumbled into the water. The bow of the workboat was still attached, leaving the boat hanging vertically. A lot of our crew was watching this maneuver as we were standing by to handle the lines. In addition, the harbor was full of other United States Navy ships with lookouts posted, binoculars and long glasses in hand—watching.

In a few minutes the block and tackle for the stern of the boat was re-attached and the crew was pulled from the water. The after end was raised level with the bow and a new crew put aboard.

The workboat was successfully lowered and motored away. The *Current* came up to our side and was made fast. With my orders in hand, I walked across a gangway, stepped aboard, and saluted the flag and the officer of the deck.

"You Jessen?" he asked. "Yes," I replied.

"I'll take your gear. The Captain wants to see you in his cabin immediately, and be careful, he's one mad S.O.B. Do you want someone to show you to his cabin?"

"No thank you, I can find it," I replied.

All salvage ships were laid out the same so I knew where the Captain's cabin was. I knocked on the Captain's door and was told to enter.

There was Captain Tiernan, seated at his desk, his head down with his hands on each side, shaking his head. He looked up at me and said, "There I was, in front of God and the United States Navy, and I dropped the boat! I dropped the boat!"

I remained silent.

He then asked, "Do you know how to raise and lower a boat?"

"Yes, sir," I responded.

"Jessen, you are now the first lieutenant. Get out there and show those monkeys how to lower a boat," he ordered.

"Yes, sir," I replied.

The Captain was a fine seaman and the crew shaped up and soon made him proud of them. But that was the most curious greeting I had ever seen.

A Brief Cure for Homesickness

O n the east coast of Korea by Pohang, in late March 1952, SCAJAP LST (Landing Ship Tank) Q030 had run aground in heavy surf. Our rescue salvage ship the USS *Current* (ARS-22) was sent to rescue them. The Japanese crew had tried to land their cargo at the tail end of a typhoon. The surf was extremely high, and the ship backed off the beach, unable to land. Unfortunately, the bow ramp was not secured properly and was left not dogged down. The sea poured into this opening and the tank deck, which was full of fifty-five-gallon drums of jet fuel, flooded. The ship partially sank as the waves pushed it towards the beach.

When our salvage crew arrived, the LST was broadside to the beach—in the worst possible position—as large waves mercilessly pounded the ship. As the salvage officer, I went aboard Q030 with a small rescue crew. Some waves hit so hard that you would be knocked down while trying to stand on the deck. We flooded all the ballast tanks to stop the ship from being further walked up the shoreline towards the beach by the huge waves—possibly destroying the ship. We relocated the Japanese crew and sent them ashore. Boy were they a happy group of sailors. My salvage crew and I slept aboard the LST.

The next day, the surf died down and our salvage ship came in close. A rope line was shot to us on board the LST from the *Current*. This line was connected to a heavy cable by a ½-inch "messenger" steel cable. This was connected to a steel cable that was 1⅝ inches in diameter. Then the 1⅝-inch cable was fastened to the LST and the *Current* slowly went out to sea, stretching the heavy cable. To the sea end of the cable, ninety feet of heavy chain was stretched out. Then a 15,000-pound anchor was dropped by the salvage ship.

On the LST, we used the ship's winch and a heavy block and tackle and pulled the bow of the ship to point seaward. This cut down on the pounding of the surf, and we knew we could now save the ship.

At dawn the next day, I awoke to hear a boat engine. It ran at full speed, and then idled, then at full speed again. I knew that something was wrong, so I raced up to the deck. There was one of my best men in a small boat, an LCVP (Landing Craft Vehicle Personnel), running in a circle. I instantly saw the problem—his rudder was jammed. The only way he could attempt to steer was to point the boat seaward and race the engine. As the boat turned toward the shore he would idle the engine. By this method he was barely keeping out of the surf.

I ran to the second LCVP, which rested in a davit over the main deck of the LST. Normally it would take ten men to launch this boat, but it was a new type of davit—where one man could lower the boat. I released the brake and the two arms that supported the bow and the stern of the LCVP slid down the overhead ramp and leaned over the side of the ship. The LCVP then was automatically lowered into the water. Like a monkey, I slid down the monkey line into the boat and got the engine started. I pulled alongside the LCVP that was in trouble. Quickly the two boats were tied together and I was able to take the other boat to safety.

After the excitement was over, I went back to the davit to admire the design that had made launching the small boat so fast and easy. There was a small nameplate fastened onto the davit. It read: Welin Davit and Boat Corporation, Perth Amboy, New Jersey. I was born in Perth Amboy, New Jersey. Being in Korea, little reminders of home made it seem like home was not so far away!

The Green Line Cruise

During the Korean War, I served aboard two rescue salvage ships. Our base was at a former Japanese Naval Yard at Sasebo, Japan. Many of the LSTs (Landing Ship Tanks) used in Korea were United States ships from World War II and had Japanese officers and crews (SCAJAP). Amphibious ships, like the very versatile LST, load and unload by pushing their bow up on unimproved beaches.

During World War II, landing craft were almost exclusively manned by Naval Reservists, who were trained in beaching—going aground. With minimal training in conventional seamanship—don't go aground—the Naval Reservists had no problem with putting landing craft, like the 328-foot-long LST, aground.

The SCAJAP crews had been trained during World War II to not go aground. This type of vessel and going aground was new to the Imperial Japanese Navy trained personnel, who had extensive training and experience in seamanship, and, incidentally, were fine sailors.

When beaching, an LST crew dropped a kedge anchor

astern, a few hundred feet off the landing area. A kedge anchor is a light anchor used to move a vessel by hauling a line attached to the anchor. When leaving, this anchor was used to help pull the LST off the beach. Sometimes the LST would back over the cable going to the kedge anchor and get the cable tangled in their propeller. To make matters worse, at times this would cause the LST to become broadside to the beach—a very dangerous location for a ship. This problem became our job; cut the cable from the screw and pull the LST off the beach.

This kept us busy and we spent a lot of time on both the east coast and west coast of Korea. One of the good things about this duty was that if you spent any month or part thereof on the coast of Korea, your earnings were income tax free. To gain this tax advantage you had to cross the "Green Line," which went around Korea.

Many of the higher ranking United States military personnel serving in Japan would board a more desirable ship than ours (a battleship, aircraft carrier, cruiser, or, if desperate, a destroyer) and travel across the "Green Line" the last day of the month and the first day of the next month to make necessary inspections. This was called the "Green Line Cruise." I was always impressed by their diligence in doing these inspections in such a "timely" manner.

CHAPTER 6

New Jersey

Winter Fresh Tomatoes

The first sanitary sewer system in Metuchen emptied into the Mill Brook at the southeast part of town. All the other raw sewage ran untreated into Dismal Swamp. During the 1930's, a sewage treatment plant was built on Jersey Avenue, and a pumping station was built on Orchard Street to pump to the new plant.

As a young boy, a group of us were given a tour of the new plant. The raw sewage was pumped into a large settling pond, circular in shape. Large revolving arms pushed anything that was floating to the edge and scraped the bottom solids to a sump. The solids were dumped into a large tank called a digester. Inside the digester, anaerobic (no oxygen) bacteria began their work. They consumed the sewage and produced methane gas, which was used to heat the facility or was flared off.

The waste water left in the pond was pumped into another circular concrete tank full of rocks. A revolving pipe trickled the water over the rocks where aerobic (oxygen) bacteria worked, producing algae on the rocks. The effluent from this tank was chlorinated and discharged into Dismal Swamp.

The sludge from the digester was pumped onto a large sand filter covered by a glass greenhouse. After the sludge was dried it was removed for fertilizer, most of which was given to local gardeners.

Now to the journey of the tomato seeds… Many of these local gardeners grew tomatoes. After a tomato was eaten, its seeds passed through the human digestive system, then the sanitary sewer system, then the digester, then they landed with the sludge on the sand filter in the greenhouse. The seeds sprouted and soon there were delicious tomatoes growing. The glass greenhouse was intended to keep the sludge from freezing in the winter but an unintended benefit was that delicious tomatoes were being grown in the greenhouse in the winter in New Jersey.

Winter tomatoes were unheard of during the 1930's. I suspect that most people were not told where these tomatoes came from.

Secaucus Garbage Recycling

Many years ago, there was an abundance of pig farms in Secaucus, New Jersey. During the summer months (in the days before air conditioning), trains heading to or from New York City had their windows wide open. The smells from the pig farms were overpowering. First time visitors to "The Garden State" had a memorable impression of a smelly state. Fortunately, New Jersey does not have to worry about that any more, assuming you ignore the scandals emanating from the state government in Trenton.

A steady stream of garbage trucks came to the pig farms. There were large concrete slabs upon which the garbage trucks dumped their loads. The adjoining pig pens were opened and the pigs strolled out and ate the garbage, rooting through the piles. After about a week, the pigs were driven back into the

pens and the remaining garbage (mostly pig manure) was loaded out and trucked to the local farms.

The Paffendorf farm was a large, local farm located on
Durham Avenue on the Metuchen-Edison boundary line. Much
of the winter was spent trucking this manure and spreading it
on the fields. A flatbed market truck was used with sideboards
on the edges. Used as a fertilizer, the pig manure produced
crops of luscious vegetables.

I was invited to lunch one day on this farm. The kitchen
had a rough wooden table with an oil-cloth covering, plain
and practical dishware, and expensive sterling silver tableware.
This was the first time I ever held a sterling silver spoon. Then
I noticed the patterns did not match. When I asked about this,
I was told that all the silverware came from the pig manure.
When people scraped their plates into the garbage sometimes a
knife, fork, or spoon tumbled in unnoticed. The farmer told me
there were four bushel baskets of sterling silver flatware out in
the barn and I could help myself.

One day a truck loaded with manure was sideswiped
by another truck. The driver did not notice that one of the
sideboards had broken and manure was flowing out onto the
roadway. When the driver arrived at the farm, the truck was
almost empty of its sloppy manure.

The farmer, being a good citizen, got a couple of men, some
brooms and shovels, and started to retrace the route. As he approached the intersection of Central and Middlesex Avenues,
he saw three state police cars, lights flashing, with the lead
trooper hanging out the police car window following the trail of
the manure. The police missed the turn onto Central Avenue
and instead went straight ahead, so they did not see the farmer.

The farmer looked at the three police cars and then turned

around and went back to the farm. Sometimes discretion is the better part of valor.

Woodbrook Farms

Woodbrook Farms was a dairy farm located in the north-west section of Raritan Township, New Jersey, south of Park Avenue. Their cows provided milk that was delivered to the local residences daily.

The milk came in glass bottles: quarts, pints, and half pints. (One nickname for smaller boys was "half pint.") The top of the bottles had a stiff paperboard cap with a tab. Over this was a glazed paper cap that covered the top inch of the bottle. It was held on with a thin wire that was soldered tightly. This prevented any tampering with the milk; tampering usually meant pouring off some of the milk and replacing it with water. The wires found many uses around our house as the 1930's were the days before twist ties.

This milk had cream in it that rose to the top. Most people would shake the bottle before using to mix in the cream. Some people would pour off the cream for their coffee or for uses in cooking.

In Metuchen public schools, when I went to kindergarten all students got a half pint of milk every day. Every week we had to bring our milk money to school, twenty-five cents, which worked out to five cents for a half pint of milk.

The delivery milkman came very early in the morning. He left the milk by the front door of your house and picked up your empty glass bottles. We never heard the term recycling; we thought it was common sense to wash out glass bottles and use them again.

In parts of New York City, up until the end of World War II, the milk wagon was pulled by horses. The horses had rubber horseshoes, in order to keep the early morning peace and quiet and not have that clop, clop, clop noise. The milkman made his deliveries by walking up to the houses. The horse did not need a driver, as he walked and followed the milkman on his route.

In the wintertime, the cows ate silage (green corn stalks chopped up and stored in silos) along with hay. In the spring-time when the cows returned to graze in the pasture, the milk would sometimes have an onion tinge from the wild onions growing in the fields.

Incidentally, there was also a breadman who delivered Dugan's Bread, which was not sliced. It had a hard crust. At dinnertime my grandfather would slice the bread by holding it against his chest. He used a large knife that he sharpened weekly on the back flagstone step.

Then someone invented sliced bread (which many people think is the best invention ever), but it just wasn't the same.

The Raccoon Hunt

I got a call from a friend of mine during the 1940's asking if I could go hunting for a raccoon with his father. My friend was sick and he did not want his father out in the woods at night by himself. So I agreed to go.

Just before sundown my friend's father pulled up in an old beat-up Ford. I got in the front seat and soon discovered four hound dogs in the back. One of them started to lick my neck.

We went out Durham Road and turned down a farm road towards Dismal Swamp. We parked and he asked if I wanted a shotgun. I said no, I would just watch.

He opened the back door and the hounds jumped out and started sniffing the ground and headed towards the swamp. It was dark, but soon a full moon appeared. The hounds started to yelp. "Come on," he said, "they have a scent! We have to follow the hounds." And so we did. Through barbed wire fences, across ditches, and across the brush covered fields of Raritan Township, New Jersey.

Suddenly the baying of the hounds changed, "They have it treed," shouted my friend's father, "Hurry up!"

We soon arrived at a wide spreading white oak tree. The hounds had their front paws on the thick tree trunk and were yelping away. The father had a large flashlight and he shined it up in the tree. After several minutes of studying the branches he said, "The raccoon is gone." He went over to the lead dog and gave it a light kick. The dog sat back and looked at the father—who made a circular motion with his hand. The dogs started to circle the tree in ever larger circles and then took off into the woods. The father explained to me that it was a smart raccoon—after climbing up the tree, it ran out on a limb and dropped to the ground. The dogs had picked up the scent again and took off as we followed. More barbed wire, sticker bushes, and ditches had to be crossed.

Then the tone of the dog's baying changed. "The dogs are in water. Hurry up! That smart old raccoon can drown the dogs!" yelled the father. We reached a small pond and the flashlight showed the raccoon pushing a dog's head under the water.

The father handed me the shotgun and waded out into the pond. He grabbed the raccoon by the neck, pulled it off the dog, shoved it underwater, and drowned it. Then he and the dogs came back to shore.

"Why didn't you shoot it?" I asked.

"I didn't want to get the raccoon meat all full of shot; besides, I could have hit the dog," was the reply.

We started back to the car and home with the dogs in the lead. I brought up the rear carrying the wet, dead raccoon. With the dogs in the back of the car and me in the front, and the dead raccoon at my feet, our hunting trip was over.

"What will you do with the raccoon?" I asked.

"I'll skin it. Have some meat for supper tomorrow and share it with the dogs. Then I'll cure the skin and make myself a coon skin hat; tail and all. By the way, do you want to go hunting again?" he asked with a sly smile.

"No thanks," I answered, "I had enough raccoon hunting to last me a lifetime."

Cabbages

New Jersey's nickname is "The Garden State." In the 1930's and 1940's many area farms trucked their produce to market and so were called "truck farms." The Paffendorf truck farm, located on Durham Road at the Metuchen-Edison border, grew all sorts of vegetables. When ready for market, the vegetables were picked, washed, packed in boxes, and loaded on a flatbed truck. It was a Ford one-and-a-half-ton truck that the farmer had lengthened to carry three tons. The load was covered with canvas and tied down.

In the late afternoon the load was taken to commission merchants in Newark, New Jersey, and New York City. I sometimes would ride in with the load.

The market in New York was particularly interesting: trucks pulling up and unloading, merchants were counting the boxes, and early buyers from the restaurants picking over the selection to get the best vegetables. One afternoon I got a call from the farmer. His driver was sick; could I take the load in? Of course I could.

When I got to the farm, the truck was loaded and the canvas cover was tied down. On top of the canvas were twenty bags of cabbages. The farmer gave me the delivery list—one stop in Newark and two in New York City. The stop in Newark was a new one so he gave me directions that would take me under a Pennsylvania Railroad Bridge.

Off I went to Newark. The road under the railroad bridge was very bumpy. I arrived at the commission merchant and backed up to unload. I was shocked and alarmed—no cabbages. After unloading I found a pay phone and called the farmer. He didn't seem too upset and said he gave me the wrong directions.

As I returned the way I came—just at the railroad bridge—the road was covered with cabbages and the citizens were gathering them up and taking them home.

About two hundred cabbages were knocked off the truck by a low bridge and the wrong directions, which made many hungry citizens very happy.

Learning the Trucking Business

Many years ago I worked for a contractor who provided trucking services. He had "borrow pits" in Woodbridge and Sayreville, New Jersey. A borrow pit is an area where a material has been dug for use at another location. The Woodbridge borrow pits were dirt, sand, and clay, which had to be separated. The Sayreville borrow pits were sand. The contractor had a few trucks of his own but mainly used other owner-operated dump trucks. He paid those owners by the cubic yard delivered.

Early one morning after his son had just returned from United States Marine Corps duty in the Korean War, his wife made both of them a nice breakfast: four eggs, bacon, and pancakes. The father drove his son to a new job so he could learn the family business.

The job was to construct a dirt road one mile long and

twenty feet wide across a salt marsh in Linden. A natural gas pipeline was to be built within the road. As the contractor and his son pulled up in their pre-war Cadillac, they saw fifteen loaded trucks parked on the road with the owner-drivers standing in a group.

"Hey, why don't you guys dump your loads and get back to work?" shouted the contractor. "We need ten cents more a yard and we aren't moving until we get it!" replied a big driver. A heated discussion ensued.

Finally the contractor addressed the crowd: "Look my kid just got home from the Marines. I'll let him settle this. You guys pick the toughest guy you got. Let him fight my kid. You throw him in the swamp, you get the ten cents. If my son throws your guy in the swamp, you all go back to work."

The biggest, meanest-looking truck driver took off his shirt and moved menacingly toward the Marine. The fight was short. The truck driver ended up in the swamp. All the truckers went back to work.

Two weeks later the contractor raised the price fifteen cents a yard. "Why?" I asked. He replied "They are all good men. I can depend on them. I want to keep them working for me."

The Hunting Preserve

In the late 1950's, my boss, Fred Arnolt was an avid hunter. He was involved with a hunting preserve that entertained businessmen by offering duck hunts and pheasant hunts. I was recruited from time to time as a "guide."

The duck hunting was done on a small pond about one acre in size. There was a blind on the south side of the pond so the shooters would not be seen by the birds.

As the "guide," I was hidden in a man-made fox hole on a hill west of the pond. In the hole with me were crates of farm-raised mallard ducks, usually two or three dozen, depending on the size of the "hunting" party.

Peeking out of the fox hole, I watched my boss for the signal (he would scratch his left ear). Then I would take a duck out of the cage and toss it up in the air. The duck, seeing the pond, would fly toward it. The "hunters" would start shooting and I would hunker down in my fox hole as the shots went in all directions, usually starting in my direction. My boss had a beautiful dog, a golden retriever, who would swim out and bring back the duck after it had been shot down. The retriever had a "soft" mouth so the duck would not be damaged. The "hunt" would last up to two hours. About half of the ducks would get away!

When the hunt was over the hunters went back to the lodge for a steak dinner. After dinner, the cleaned and frozen ducks from the previous week's hunting party were given to the triumphant hunters to take home.

On other days there would be a pheasant hunt. The pheasants were raised on site and then released to live in the surrounding fields. There were feeding stations to keep them healthy.

There would be three or four hunters, including my boss. They would walk in line abreast across the field with dogs to scare up the pheasants. Another "guide" and I would be at the ends of the line behind the hunters.

Each guide had two pheasants under his coat with the pheasant's heads tucked under their arms. If no birds were kicked up by the advancing line, my boss would yell, "Over there! On the right!" Then the left guide would take out one pheasant and toss it up in the air. The shotgun barrels swung around and the guides hit the dirt. Some of these shooters were very dangerous. Many pheasants got away too!

After the hunt, the hunters went back to the lodge for a steak dinner. After dinner, cleaned and frozen pheasants from the previous week's hunt were given to the hunters to take home.

Incidentally, the birds were usually loaded with birdshot, which is bad for your teeth.

The Great Beds Lighthouse

If you go to the waterfront in Perth Amboy, New Jersey, and look out to the east, you will see a white lighthouse with a black bottom. This is the Great Beds Lighthouse. It is located on the east end of the Great Beds. Who slept in the Great Beds? Oysters! Raritan Bay once had a thriving oyster industry with large sailboats to drag the oyster rakes.

It is important that lighthouses have a unique physical appearance for daytime sightings and that their light has a specific characteristic for nighttime identification. When the mariner sights a lighthouse it is *very* important that he knows which one it is, so he can match it up with the chart. That is why their shapes, coloring, and lights are different.

The Great Beds Lighthouse (operational in 1880) was first lit with kerosene. The lighthouse keeper and his family lived in the lighthouse. He had to maintain the light and wind the machinery that made the light flash. Lighthouses had flashing lights, which flash on, or occulting lights, which flash off. Today, the Great Beds Lighthouse light is electric, automatic, and unmanned.

A wooden boat hung in davits off the side of the lighthouse and was rowed back and forth to Perth Amboy. Imagine rowing in twice a day for the kids to go to school! That's three and a half miles of rowing each school day. Most of the supplies were delivered by steam-powered vessels of the lighthouse service. Coal was used for heat in the winter.

On 2 January 1918, Raritan Bay was frozen over. My wife's father, Willard Lynn Bruner, drove his Model T Ford onto the ice and parked it by the lighthouse. Happily we have a picture of him in the car with the lighthouse in the background and ice skaters gliding by.

Where Did The Great Beds Go?

The New Jersey Turnpike was built from 1950 to 1952. Certain northern sections went over marsh wetlands where the muddy marsh material was up to fifty feet deep and could not support the roadway. One plan was to build a bridge over the marsh, but that would have been too expensive.

Instead, an ingenious solution was implemented. The first step was to cover the right of way for the turnpike roadway with four to five feet of sand—a porous material. This formed the work platform. Pile drivers were brought in and large pipe piles were driven down through the marsh. The bottom of these piles had a trap door. The driven piles were filled with sand. Compressed air was applied to the top of the sand so it stayed in place as the pile was removed. This created a sand wick through the muddy material.

Steel plates were placed at regular intervals along the roadway and two-inch pipes were welded to the plates to stand vertically to measure the settlement of the roadway.

Then layers of fill were brought in to overload the roadway. With the extra weight of the fill, the sand platform began to weep water at the edges. The idea was to squeeze the water out of the muddy marsh material to consolidate it to support the roadway. Speed was important, but not too fast or the vertical sand drains would plug up with mud. I went to look at the site and the clear water was draining really fast—like a spring wicking out of the side of the sand work platform.

The overload was completed to twice the future load (the estimated weight of the roadway itself and traffic). The survey parties continued to check the settlement via the measurements on the vertical pipes welded to the steel plates. The squeezing out of the water lasted for several months until the settlement was complete. Then the overload was spread out for the sides (shoulders) of the roadway.

Now back to the Great Beds—the shallow oyster beds in Raritan Bay between Perth Amboy and Staten Island. Dredges were brought in and the sandy material of the Great Beds was loaded into bottom-dump barges. Tugboats took the barges up to waterways near the turnpike and the material was bottom-dumped into the water. Then another dredge pumped the material to the turnpike. Other areas of New York Harbor were also dredged to create fill material.

The dredging also improved navigation and the site of the Great Beds became what it is today—an anchorage area for ships and barges. Next time you travel the New Jersey Turnpike, appreciate the smooth ride and think of how sand from the Great Beds helped build the turnpike.

Chicken Manure

In the 1950's, I moved into a split-level house on Bryant Avenue in a new development, called North View Acres, located by Metuchen High School. In a few years I decided to start a garden. The topsoil was a little tired.

In the winter when the ground was frozen and there was four inches of snow, I spread two pickup truckloads of fresh chicken manure on the garden as a fertilizer. You have to be careful with fresh chicken manure because it's "HOT."

Two days later there was a warm spell and our backyard had a flock of preschool children actively picking up chicken feathers. They were having a great time and I thought everything was OK. I soon found out I was wrong. I received several phone calls from irate mothers wanting to know what that brown stuff was on their child's boots and snowsuits. I explained organic gardening to them, but it kind of fell flat.

Spring came; we plowed the garden and started planting. The first crop was radishes. They were bright red with green tops. We picked them, washed them, and tied them into bunches.

My four-year-old son "Skippy," Martin Andrew Jessen, loaded up his wagon and started around the neighborhood giving out the radishes. At one house he rang the doorbell. The women of the house asked him in. Several ladies were visiting and admired the radishes. "How do you grow them to be so nice?" they asked.

My son proudly held up the bright red bunch and said, "It's the chicken manure that does it!"

Timed Tests

A friend of mine was an experienced professor at Rutgers—The State University of New Jersey. He was asked to monitor an important test and was given instructions on how to give the test.

He entered a room with over sixty students. He introduced himself and explained the test rules. The test was to be timed to thirty minutes. Blue test booklets would be passed out and kept closed until the start signal was given. After thirty minutes, "time" would be called. Then all booklets were to be closed and turned in immediately.

When the thirty minutes were up, he called, "time," and the students began putting the booklets on his desk. At the back of the room one student was feverously writing. "Time is up," called the professor, "you are three minutes overtime."

The student came forward and spoke in a threatening manner, "Do you know who I am?" "No," replied the professor. The student picked up half the pile of test booklets, slipped his in the middle, and walked out.

When my friend told me this story, I asked what he did. "I gave him three minutes extra for ingenuity," he replied with a big smile.

Ducks and Scurvy

For over forty years we have had ducks in the ponds behind our office on Main Street in Metuchen, New Jersey. Generations of mothers have brought their children to "see the ducks." The ducks lay eggs and sometimes they hatch out, depending on the local raccoons.

Years ago, eight healthy ducklings hatched. I arrived at work one morning when they were two weeks old. I saw that they could not stand up. They tried but tumbled over. Someone suggested that I call the "duck man" at Middlesex County Parks.

I felt silly but I made the call and asked for the "duck man."

A gentleman answered and said he was the "duck man." I explained my problem.

"What are you feeding them?" he asked.

"Cracked corn and the kids feed them white bread," I replied.

"That's your problem. They are filling up on the white bread and not getting enough vitamins. They have scurvy. Go to a feed store and get regular duck food that has all the vitamins."

We got the duck food, fed it to the ducklings, and the next morning they were running around.

I called the "duck man" and told him of our success. His comment was that white bread should only be used to pick up broken glass. Kids deserve better.

Sailors on long voyages would get scurvy—a deficiency in vitamin C (ascorbic acid). The British Navy solved this by giving everyone lime juice. They carried barrels of it. That's why they were called "Limeys."

How We Got Trees in Downtown Metuchen

Many years ago we thought the downtown Metuchen, New Jersey, shopping area would look nicer if it had some trees. I got three nice eight-by-ten photos taken from the Pennsylvania Railroad Bridge looking north right down the center line of Main Street. An artist friend of mine took one copy and painted in an initial planting of trees, and then took a second copy and painted in trees ten years later. I thought we were on our way.

A citizen who was running for town council took these pictures as part of his political platform. He lost the election. The trees were a dead issue. Several times I talked to the local politicians about Main Street trees. They always smiled at me and said they liked the idea, but soon I came to realize that their answer was an unspoken, "No."

Years went by with no trees. One spring day Ernie Hammesfahr, a Metuchen businessman, came to me and said, "Let's plant some trees downtown."

I explained the sad history to him.

But Ernie said, "I'll get ten people to donate one hundred and fifty dollars for a tree—fifty dollars for the tree and one hundred for the hole." Soon cutouts were made in the sidewalks and one day we had instant trees. As far as I know, no official permission was given, this just happened. I guess Ernie got the right people to donate.

In later years the Metuchen Chamber of Commerce added additional trees to the downtown area. This is how we got our beautiful trees downtown.

The Cannon

A talented friend of mine, R. Bruce McDowell, owned a machine shop where he purchased a new metal turning lathe. Since he was interested in guns, he at once got the idea to build a cannon. After doing some research, he bought a large piece of brass and some antique twenty-eight-inch wooden wheels with iron bands around them. Construction of the cannon began.

The twenty-seven-inch barrel was a turning and boring job, but the major challenge was making the trunnions. Trunnions are the knobs on each side of the cannon that let the barrel swing up and down for aiming purposes. Normally they are part of the casting when the metal is poured for the barrel. In this case, the trunnions had to be turned in a lathe, threaded on the ends, then the barrel bored and tapped on the sides to receive the trunnions. A true stroke of genius was to line the threads with silver solder, tighten the trunnions, and then apply heat to melt the solder into the threads. This yielded a tight seal to contain the force of the explosion of the gunpowder.

With all the metal work done, a carriage to hold the cannon was built out of solid oak wood. After many hours of hard work the cannon was now complete. There was only one thing more to do—try out the cannon. Bruce wheeled his brand new cannon outside behind his shop, put half a pint of gunpowder down the barrel, stuffed the barrel with wads of toilet paper, and fired it.

Unfortunately, it was wintertime and the large white oak tree behind the shop still clung to its dry, brown leaves. With a large roar, the flaming paper wadding flew up into the oak tree and set the leaves on fire! Then the excitement really started. Fire trucks rushed to the scene with sirens blaring followed by police cars with lights flashing. Next, the first aid squad ambulance arrived.

As for the fire, it was spectacular, but it soon burned out.

However, fire was still in the eyes of the policemen. Did my friend Bruce know that it was illegal to discharge firearms within the Borough of Metuchen, New Jersey? Arrest was imminent.

Then Bruce's wife Dorothy came to the rescue—with a dictionary. A firearm is a weapon that can be carried. No one could carry the cannon. Case closed.

Optimistic Reading

When cold winter winds blow the snow about, I like to indulge myself in the ultimate optimism—seed catalogues. Winter, it's that time of year when seed catalogs start arriving. They are probably one of the most optimistic things around (except for that latest tip on the stock market).

I like to study the vegetables first. The beautiful colored pictures let me imagine how they will look in the garden at harvest time. Then I study the descriptions of each vegetable along with their growing times.

I am mostly into vegetables. I have my favorites. I know I will plant broccoli, peas, beans, lettuce, spinach, and tomatoes. There are many varieties of tomatoes. I stick to the indeterminate types, called "vining tomatoes," that climb over six feet along my arbor. The determinate types, called "bush tomatoes," grow in a more compact plant that is approximately four feet high.

My favorite tomato is—the Rutgers tomato. The scientifically bred Rutgers tomato was introduced in 1934 as a general use to-mato for canning, juicing, and the fresh market. During a time of commercial expansion of the canning business and truck farming in New Jersey, the Rutgers tomato was a good perform-ing tomato for New Jersey's many processors: Campbell, Heinz, Hunt, and others. It is no longer grown commercially but still popular for home gardeners.

A few years ago my Rutgers tomatoes came in very late—perhaps due to problems with the football stadium. And last year the Rutgers tomatoes didn't do well—I think it was caused by the sadness over their football team's record.

I do crop rotation with tomatoes and lima beans. The lima beans put nitrogen into the soil, the tomatoes take it out.

My favorite beet is called "Long Season." They grow bigger than baseballs and are sweet and tender.

Potatoes are fun to grow. When you harvest them it is like looking for buried treasure. I am usually able to dig them up all the way into February. "Yukon Gold" potatoes are very good.

One year I had a groundhog problem. This hungry fellow was eating my beans and broccoli. Alas, he was hit by a car while crossing to a neighbor's garden. I scooped him up and buried him near an apple tree. I marked the grave with three squash seeds. The seeds grew and the vines headed for the ap-ple tree. Up they climbed. That fall, my apple tree provided a bumper crop of squash, all from just one groundhog!

It is fun, healthy, and good exercise to have a garden, but it is also fun to study the seed catalogs. It feels good to sit in a warm house, with a cold wind blowing outside and dream of the harvest to come. Try it. Dreaming is important.

Dear Deer

As an avid gardener I have always seen small animals come into my garden to get a good meal. This year I saw something in my backyard that I had never seen before. Two deer were munching on my grass—a buck and a doe. I went outside to look and they jumped over the four-foot fence with ease.

I started planting my vegetable garden this spring. A double row of beans twenty feet long soon sprouted and the leaves began to form. The next day it looked like a lawn mower had gone down my rows of beans. I blamed the groundhog who lived under my shed, but he soon left. More of my other vegetables were eaten and I saw deer footprints. I realized that the groundhog was falsely accused. Then the deer ate the green tops of my beets and then munched on the part of the beet that was the root portion.

Next, two very cute fawns appeared. It took me almost ten minutes to chase them out of the garden. What will they eat in Metuchen when the winter comes?

I noticed the deer rubbing against the brush. I was shocked! They have ticks! Deer ticks crawl out to the tips of the leaves and branches and attach themselves to humans to suck their blood. I am a human. Deer ticks are a source of Lyme disease, a disease that is hard to detect as it mimics other diseases.

One of my relatives got Lyme disease and all her joints locked up and her knees swelled. Thank God she is better now. If not treated promptly Lyme disease can cause chronic joint inflammation as well as impaired memory. Even if one is cured, it can attack again when your body's defenses are low. So I want the deer to stay away!

Should the government protect us from Lyme disease and all the car accidents that the surplus deer cause? I have the solution; it's very simple and only one word—venison!

CHAPTER 7

Church Stories

Bringing Back a Stream of Memories

I n Metuchen, New Jersey, as I pass the corner of Amboy and Graham Avenues I see a vacant lot where the old wooden Reformed Church, built in 1858, once stood. In 1946, a painter was using a blowtorch to remove old paint from a lower window frame near the base of the steeple. Looking up, he noticed smoke coming out of the steeple, and then flames. Unfortunately, the church was built with balloon framing with studs running all the way from the bottom to the top, which created a series of small chimneys inside the walls. Soon the church itself was on fire.

The Metuchen Fire Department responded, but the fire was too much for them. The old pump trucks could not get the water pressure high enough to get to the height of the flames. The church was a total loss. Metuchen bought two new fire trucks after the fire.

The Reformed Church temporarily held worship services in the Forum Theater building. The Forum Theater had a theatre organ that was designed to accompany silent films. The theatre organ had many unusual items: bells, whistles, drums, and castanets. It even had a siren.

Within a year of the fire, a new brick church was built on Lake Avenue in Metuchen. The church is blessed with a large pipe organ that came from another church that had been demolished. This organ is very big, with over fifty ranks. There are over three thousand pipes in the rooms behind the curtains at the front of the church. I love to hear this organ play the old familiar hymns.

In 1781, at the Revolutionary War Battle of Springfield, New Jersey, the Patriots ran out of paper wadding for their guns. Their flintlock muskets, loaded with powder and ball, required a paper wadding to keep the ball tight against the powder and prevent the ball from rolling out if the barrel was lowered.

The local minister came out of the church carrying hymn books written by Isaac Watts (1674 – 1748). As he tore the pages out of the hymn book he shouted to the American troops, "Give them Watts boys! Give them Watts!" Our church hymn book still contains twelve hymns written by Isaac Watts, including "Joy to the World."

Another thought of mine about hymns is the memory of a thousand sailors at Great Lakes Naval Training Center boot camp singing the Navy Hymn in 1944. Or in 1951 in Sasebo, Japan, as around one hundred sailors sang the Navy Hymn in a Quonset hut just before we were to board our ships to head for Korea and into an oncoming typhoon. The lyrics were written by William Whiting in 1860 and the music by Reverend John Bacchus Dykes in 1861. The words of the first verse of this hymn are forever etched in my mind:

> Eternal Father, strong to save,
> Whose arm hath bound the restless wave,
> Who bidd'st the mighty ocean deep
> Its own appointed limits keep;
> O hear us when we cry to Thee,
> For those in peril on the sea.

Attend the services of your faith. It will be good for you, good for your community, and good for our nation.

The Parsonage Committee

In the midst of the Great Depression, at the age of nine, my mother, Hannah Hughes Jessen, dragged me off to a meeting of the parsonage committee that was to be held at the minister's house on Home Street in Metuchen, New Jersey. Money was short and the Methodist Church was on a tight budget. My mother's instructions to me were to be silent, listen carefully, and watch the faces of the speakers, you will learn something.

There were four other women on the committee; the minister's wife was not present. The first item of discussion was the problem with the rug in the room we were meeting in. The "line of march" on the rug was worn down to the backing. The first suggestion was to turn the rug. Some previous group had already thought of that as the rest of the rug was equally worn because of being turned.

Now the discussion went to a smaller rug to cover the distressed portion, but this was rejected as a tripping hazard. The discussion heated up. It seemed that the present rug had been partially worn out in someone's house before being donated to the parsonage.

Then the use of the room was discussed. Although it was customary for the minister to visit each family at least once a year, some people came to the parsonage for personal matters. Therefore, the condition of the room reflected on the church.

I noticed that my mother was silent while the rest talked. When people started to repeat previous thoughts my mother spoke up, summarized the conversation, and maneuvered the group towards a solution. My mother then said, "Let's buy a new rug." A unanimous vote followed for a brand new rug.

Finally, the woman who lived next door asked, "What about the clothespin problem?" She explained that when hanging the wash out to dry, it was customary to pin one end of the first piece, then the next pin held the other end and the second piece. So that ten pieces of wash would take eleven pins. The minister's wife put two pins on each piece, using twenty clothespins for ten pieces of wash.

Then the discussion went to who should tell the minister's wife of her improper use of clothespins. I could see my mother was getting disgusted about the committee getting involved in such a trivial matter. "My goodness, don't you know that extra clothespins let the wash dry faster! I'm going home," said my mother. I learned I had to be very careful with my mom.

The Spaghetti Supper

The Methodist Church was formerly on the corner of Main Street and Middlesex Avenue, Metuchen, New Jersey, across from the Borough Hall. A wooden church was built in

1866 and in 1917 a masonry structure was added. In the 1950's, the congregation built a new church at the end of Hillside Avenue—a more secluded location. The old church was used as a theater and then was torn down and replaced by a bank.

During the 1930's, Metuchen's merchants stayed open until nine o'clock on Friday nights. There was a variety of stores: grocery, butcher, hardware, radio, shoe, shoemaker, hats, clothing, newspaper, stationary, drug, florists, confectionary, ice cream, jewelry, tailor, furniture, and candy.

The Methodist Church men's club decided to have a Friday night spaghetti supper. As a young boy, I was to help set up tables and chairs and be generally useful. The pots were boiling in the church kitchen and wonderful smells were coming out.

About four thirty in the afternoon, the men came into the dining area talking about a serious problem. Only thirty tickets had been sold and they had figured on hosting over one hundred people. Just then an older man came in. I knew he was rich. I helped take the collection in church and he always put a ten dollar bill in the plate. Most people put in change and maybe a few put in one dollar.

"What's wrong?" he asked, noticing the forlorn faces.

"We sold only thirty tickets," was the reply.

"I am a salesman," said the older man "Give me a bunch of tickets. When do you start serving?"

"Five o'clock," was the reply.

He left and we all went back to cooking. At five o'clock we opened the door and about fifteen people came in. We served them as a steady stream of customers began to come in. By six o'clock we went out to get more food, and I was busy washing dishes. Spaghetti was served until after seven. The salesman came back. We asked how he sold so many tickets.

He replied, "I went up the street, stopping in every store saying that there is a spaghetti supper at the Methodist Church. It's a short walk and quick service. You have to eat, so why not eat there? Then I worked on the store customers."

Over two hundred dinners were sold. I was amazed that one man could do so much so fast. I know now that he had several helpers: ambition, enthusiasm, a smile, and, a love of people can accomplish amazing things.

Later that year he moved to Florida. He and his wife bought a trailer, joined a carnival, and spent eight months a year "on the road" selling fancy kitchen gadgets.

He did not need the money. He just liked to sell things.

Sunday School

In the late 1940's, I was Sunday school superintendant at the Methodist Church in Metuchen, New Jersey. This was when television was only in the evening and during the rest of the day a test pattern was on the television, which some of us watched.

Many children had been arriving late to Sunday school. To solve this problem, a sixteen-millimeter sound movie projector was purchased and an arrangement was made with a store in Perth Amboy that had a film library to rent a cartoon every week. Besides Mickey Mouse, there was Bugs Bunny, Woody Wood Pecker, Looney Tunes, Popeye the Sailor, and many others.

Sunday school started on time with a cartoon. Tardiness

evaporated. Total attendance increased dramatically. I knew we were doing the right thing when parents objected that the children were pestering them to get to Sunday school early. In a few cases some of the younger children learned to tell time.

I recruited teachers in June for the September opening. One year I was warned about a problem—a very rambunctious class coming out of the primary department. I recruited one of our church members who managed the Personnel Department (Human Resources) at a very large employer. I explained the challenge of the class. He had a master's degree in education and was confident he could handle the class.

In September, the "trouble class" started with an uproar. I thought a master's degree could take care of that, but it did not. For the cartoon, his class sat on benches that had a large over-hang at each end. The class filled the bench with the teacher sitting on the end overhang. When the cartoon flashed "The End" all the children stood together; the bench flipped up de-positing the teacher on the floor. He quit.

A week earlier an older woman offered to teach a class or be a substitute. She told me she had not finished high school but that she knew her Bible well and liked kids. I filed her name with the notation "*her* Bible and likes kids."

I called her. She accepted and asked for a list of the chil-dren. I offered to tell her about the troublemakers. She said she didn't want to know. The next Sunday things went well but I thought that was because of the newness of the teacher.

The following Sunday I noticed the class made sure she sat in the middle of the bench for the cartoon. After that I knew ev-erything was all right. Teaching is a gift like the ability to dance; although she did not have a degree, she was a born teacher.

The Sunday school room was now getting a lot of use and it

soon needed a paint job. I borrowed some tall ladders and scaf-folding, and had volunteers ready to paint.

Then the trouble began. What color do we paint the room? A meeting was called. The discussion turned nasty; I had not thought that nice people could be so mean over the color of a room.

A senior church member called out for order. He announced that as a church democracy it was only fair that everyone should have some influence on the color. He suggested everyone bring in a gallon of the paint color they wanted the room painted. It would then be mixed together and the resulting color used. There was total silence after this proposal. Some people began to leave. Those who remained said, "You pick the color."

I learned some old guys are pretty smart and that Democracy works, at least for paint.

The Bishop's Speech

Long ago we had a personnel problem at the Methodist Church in Metuchen, New Jersey. A church meeting of all the members was called and the bishop came and presided over the meeting. The meeting started with a sense that the problem was caused by the bishop. He was aware of that as he gave a short sermon entitled "Things don't always turn out the way you want or expect."

He told of giving a commencement address at a college. As he walked into the building, he realized that he had forgotten his prepared speech. As he opened the door to the large auditorium where he was to give his speech, he saw in big bronze letters the word "PUSH" on the door. He was inspired and decided to make his speech about that important word.

The bishop began by saying, "Today I want to talk to you about a four letter word that can help you throughout your entire life. This four letter word, properly applied can solve problems, overcome obstacles, and help you get ahead in life. It just so happens that this four letter word is emblazoned just over the bronze handles of the door of this auditorium. All the students turned around and there was the four letter word "PULL" written on the door.

The church audience laughed at the bishop's college mistake. He continued, "Ladies and gentlemen as to our problem today. Things don't always work out the way you want. The problem is my fault. Now let's see what we can do to fix it." Fix it he did.

I realized that this was a smart man. He made mistakes and admitted them. The meeting could have developed into squabbles and much unhappiness. Instead he told a story of one of his mistakes, shouldered all the blame, and left a lot of us a little wiser.

Thomas Pond

Thomas Pond was given to the town of Metuchen, New Jersey, in 1929 by the grandchildren of David Graham

Thomas. David Graham Thomas owned a lot of real estate and was like the "Donald Trump" of Metuchen in the second half of the nineteenth century. Graham Avenue and Thomas Street were named after him. For many years his surviving relatives would remind us that it was Thomas Pond, not Tommy's Pond. Miss Bogart, our librarian many years ago, would often remind me, "Remember Martin, its Thomas Pond, not Tommy's Pond."

When I was a kid, Thomas Pond was a great place for frogs. We would catch them but it was difficult. In the spring, there were lots of pollywogs. It was fun to watch them grow. First the hind legs appeared, then the front legs, and then the tail began to shrink, and, suddenly, there were the new frogs!

At nighttime you could hear the really big bullfrogs croaking away.

Years later, one Easter Sunday, I was at the door of the Reformed Church that overlooks the pond. As the parishioners left the church, I was busy taking notes for the minister so he could remember the names of people who wanted visiting or counseling. My seven-year-old daughter, in her new Easter coat, told me she was going down to the pond. A few minutes later she returned triumphantly showing me a snail the size of a ping pong ball.

"Look what I found!" Nancy exclaimed, proudly holding up the muddy dripping snail. As I admired it she added, "And look! I have both pockets of my coat full of more snails!"

Then her mother arrived. This was not a happy time.

CHAPTER 8

Strictly Business

Summer Jobs

In 1949, the year between my junior and senior years at Rutgers University, I needed a summer job. The previous two summers I had worked at Rutgers in the Engineering and Soils Research Laboratory. It was now time for me to get into the real world.

Borrowing the family car, I drove my dad to work, and then drove around searching for a job. In those days you looked for the job, instead of the job looking for you.

Route 100, which became part of the New Jersey Turnpike, was being built, so I went out to one of the bridge construction sites. I received a courteous reception, but no job offer. As I left, a senior highway department engineer called me over. "Cheer up," he said, "What do you have to offer besides a strong back and a weak mind?" I told him, "Three years of Rutgers civil engineering, two summers of soils lab, plus two years in the United States Navy." He got more serious now as he replied, "Get back into your car. Everyplace you see a construction job-site, stop and ask to speak to the boss. By the time the sun goes down, you will have a job."

He was right. On U.S. Route 1 in Edison, New Jersey, just west of Main Street, a huge factory for producing floor coverings was being built. I was offered a summer job by the general contractor, Del Webb Construction from Las Vegas, Nevada. I would work in the survey party as a rodman and chainman.

This was a great opportunity, as this job would take me all over this vast construction project; from the bottom of the trenches for the footings, to the top of the structural steel. It was a great chance to learn all sorts of things. The job was a union construction project, and that would be another part of my education.

Except for the two water boys, I was the youngest person on the jobsite. In those days boys still delivered water to over a hundred workmen from an open bucket with a common dipper. I learned that Del Webb was a super rich guy who got his start by building The Flamingo (a casino in Las Vegas) owned by Bugsy Siegel. Del Webb was also an owner of the New York Yankees baseball team.

One rainy day our three-man survey party was in the office shanty doing the layout computations for a series of railroad sidings. We had no computers—just a slide rule, log tables, and a hand-cranked adding machine to calculate a series of angles and distances to lay out the switches and curves of the railroad yard.

In the shanty next door was the jobsite superintendent's office, where a shouting match between the superintendent and the head of the bricklayers union was going on. This job was going to be a huge bricklaying job. The plans showed steel frame buildings completely enclosed with bricks. For the bricklayers union, this job represented work for over one hundred men for months. The problem was that the union wanted to limit the number of bricks that each man could lay in a day. The production rate that they chose was half the production rate that nonunion bricklayers out in Nevada were doing on other Del Webb construction jobs.

We heard the voices calm down, and then the union man left. The teletype machine to Las Vegas began sounding off. To make a long story short, two weeks later, the sides of the buildings were changed from brick to insulated steel. Instead of months and thousands of bricklayer man-hours, the siding was put up in sixty days by fourteen ironworkers. The only brickwork on the whole job was a small office building, which was work for only a handful of bricklayers. I learned that if you ask for too much, sometimes you get a lot less or nothing at all.

One day, Del Webb himself was coming to the jobsite for an inspection, and everyone was so excited. Imagine an owner of the New York Yankees on our jobsite! Unfortunately, a problem developed at the jobsite in the afternoon before his arrival. During one of the concrete pours some of the bracing failed, which caused the wooden wall-forms to shift, resulting in a bent wall. This obvious error would have to be removed. Del Webb's tour of the jobsite was carefully laid out to miss this problem wall. However, when he heard the jackhammers breaking up the wall, he headed right to it. The superintendent expected a first class chewing out as they looked at the problem wall, and Del Webb said, "Your bracing failed."

The superintendent's face showed pain, then fear, as he seemed to shrink before our eyes. Del Webb noticed this too. He put his arm around the superintendent and spoke in a loud voice so the considerable audience could hear as he said, "That same problem happened to me many times. Now let's go see more of this jobsite." Instead of beating up the superintendent he brought himself down to our level, or did he raise us up to his level?

I remembered what my father, Martin Jessen, once told me: "When you yell at someone and ball them out, enjoy that moment to the fullest. Because that moment will be the only 'good' that will ever come out of it."

I learned many valuable lessons working in construction during my summer job.

Frugality

Years ago I worked for a wealthy man who owned a piece of land that was mined for sand and dirt—what we called a "borrow pit." This wealthy man said he bought land by the acre and sold it by the truckload.

I was employed to do estimating for him. He always insisted that I calculate on both sides of each piece of paper fully—no wasted paper!

One of the tools I used was a hand-operated adding machine that printed on a paper tape. One morning I put an empty waste basket by my desk and I let the tape pile up inside the waste basket. At the end of the work day, I rolled the tape backwards onto the roller.

My employer asked, "What are you doing?"

I replied, "Tomorrow I will use the other side of the tape."

The next morning my employer had an empty waste basket next to his desk that caught his adding machine tape too!

Good Business

In the 1950's, Smith Tractor was the local Caterpillar dealer and was owned by two brothers: E. Smith, the salesman, and Fred Smith, the mechanic. The company was fairly large and had about forty employees.

One day I was talking to E. Smith about buying a D8 bulldozer. At that time there was a waiting list to purchase them. A beat-up pickup truck pulled up alongside of us with a woman with a baby on the passenger side. A very anxious looking young man leaped out of the driver's side and rushed up towards us. E. Smith introduced me to this young man. The young man said he had a job to dig out ten basements and his bulldozer had just broken down. He needed it fixed right away but unfortunately he had no money.

E. Smith said in a calming voice, "Let's go and see Fred. We can worry about the money later." Back in the shop we met Fred, who had grease-stained overalls and very dirty hands. The bulldozer problem was described in detail by the young man. Fred explained how to fix it. Fred went to the parts counter and got the needed parts. Then he went into his personal toolbox and took out a special tool. Fred said to the young man, "You will need this tool. Please bring it back when you are done."

I watched as E. Smith went to the pickup truck where he talked to the wife, admired the baby, wished them good luck, and sent them on their way. I was so moved by this scene that I said, "That was very nice of you and Fred, how you took care of that family."

E. Smith smiled and said to me, "Marty that was just good business. That young fellow is a hard worker, totally honest, and his wife keeps the books and is very good with money. In three or four years they will have ten or twelve machines, all made by Caterpillar. In fifteen or sixteen years from now that baby will be learning to operate a Caterpillar machine."

I drove home thinking: "Did I just see two very nice guys or did I just see two very shrewd businessmen, or both?"

Pollution Solution

In the 1950's, we did an interesting construction job in Wind Gap, Pennsylvania. The job was for a major petroleum company which needed to modify an abandoned slate quarry in order to store gasoline there. Gasoline requires a floating roof tank to prevent evaporation. The wall of the quarry was smoothed out for about ten feet where the roof could move up and down and keep the seal.

To start the operation, the quarry was filled with water with the roof floating at the proper elevation. Gasoline came into the quarry via a pipeline. The gasoline floated on top of the water—gasoline and water don't mix.

Whenever gasoline came in, at the same time, water was pumped out into an adjoining quarry. This kept the floating roof in balance and maintained the seal.

Whenever gasoline was removed, water was pumped back in

from the adjacent quarry to keep the roof even with the smooth part of the wall. It was a balancing act, and it worked. This quarry held as much gasoline as a very large steel tank field.

The water in the adjacent quarry was crystal clear, but there was a problem. A rainbow sheen appeared on the surface of the adjacent pond; a small amount of gasoline could make a lot of sheen. No problem, there are bacteria that could control that. After all, it was a closed system with all the water staying on site, and no water being dumped into a stream.

Soon the scientists came to put the bacteria in the balancing quarry pond. They made several attempts over many weeks with negative results.

An Amish farmer sat in his horse-drawn wagon watching their most recent attempt. He got down off his wagon and asked the scientists what they were doing. The scientists explained.

The farmer scratched his chin and said, "You know them bacteria need something to eat. Look how clear the water is."

The scientist said, "The bacteria are to eat the gasoline sheen."

He scratched his chin again and said, "You don't just eat meat, you like vegetables with it."

"What do we use for vegetables?" asked the scientist.

"Horse manure," was the reply, "and I can get you a wagon load in two hours. I'll charge you five dollars."

The horse manure was purchased and shoveled into the water. In two weeks the water turned green with thriving bacteria. The sheen disappeared. The bacteria were happy, the scientists ecstatic, and the farmer had a customer for a load of manure every year.

Sometimes a little pollution is the solution.

The Forum Theater

In the 1930's we had movies six days a week. Sunday was for church. At the Forum Theater in Metuchen, New Jersey, there were two evening shows: the first starting at seven o'clock and the second at nine o'clock. The charge was fifteen cents for children and twenty-five cents for adults. Saturday there was an afternoon matinee, ten cents for children and fifteen cents for adults. Remember, this was when a hamburger at White Castle was five cents.

Each show began with a newsreel followed by a cartoon or other short, and then the main picture. There was a candy machine, five cents for a candy bar or a box of Good & Plenty licorice. If you rode your bicycle, you could park it in the lobby.

Some evenings my Sunday school teacher, Mr. Faroat, would invite me to listen to him play the organ at the Forum. This was a theatre organ, not like a church organ. It was designed to accompany silent pictures. In addition to regular organ pipes there were sound effects: snare drum, base drum, castanets, train whistle, and siren, to name a few.

My Sunday school teacher would start playing twenty minutes before the movie. He could not read music but that didn't seem to bother him. He was good. The fringe benefit was that I could stay and see the movie for free.

If you go to Radio City Music Hall in New York City, especially the Christmas show, they have a huge Wurlitzer theatre organ with two independently working consoles. We used to go to Radio City to see a movie plus the stage show. There were always long lines on Saturdays when we went. If we couldn't get in, we would go to the nearby Roxy Theatre to see a movie and stage show. Roxy designed Radio City and started the famous line of female precision dancers—"The Roxyettes" (now called "The Rockettes").

In the 1950's, my Sunday school teacher was a member of a theatre organ society. They played at the Rahway Theater. In 1960, they learned that the Roxy Theatre was to be torn down. It was owned by the developer that originally built Menlo Park Shopping Center. The society contacted him and he arranged for them to spend a whole day playing the great organ there.

Today there are many amusements to take up our time, but let me tell you, it was just great to go to the movie theaters with their organs and stage shows.

Proper Attire

I n the last century, I earned my living in the site preparation and excavating business. It might seem like dirt to you, but it was bread and butter to me. Our company, Arnolt Bros, Inc., prepared sites for people to live at and to work at. We prepared sites for schools for their children and we prepared sites for the roads to connect everything. We installed pipes to bring people water and to take water away. It was a good business and I was always proud that our efforts made people's lives better.

We once submitted a bid for a very large site job for a major corporation. A few days after the bid was in, I got a call on my two-way radio stating that this major corporation wanted to talk to me in one hour in New York City. I was out at a jobsite at the time with muddy boots, grease stains on my pants, and generally was disreputable looking. It was a must meeting with no time to change. I jumped into my station wagon and drove to New York.

I arrived at the company headquarters and was ushered into a large plush conference room. I had my muddy boots in one hand and a newspaper in the other. Just inside the door I spread the paper and sat my boots down.

There were over a dozen men waiting for me, all with suits and ties on. Plans were laid out on the table and, after introductions, the questions started. It was a difficult dirt moving job and I explained the potential problems and offered some ideas of how to solve them. After an hour's discussion I was dismissed. I drove back to my office in Metuchen, New Jersey, disgusted with myself for having blown-it.

At the office everyone wanted to know if we got the job. I explained my lack of proper attire and told everyone that I thought I had failed. That same day at five o'clock in the afternoon we got a call from the architect requesting me to meet him at the Holiday Inn. When I met him, he handed me a letter of intent and said they wanted me to move bulldozers onto the jobsite the next day. I was shocked and asked him, "Why did you choose us from so many bidders on this project?"

The architect said, "You looked like an excavator, you acted like an excavator, and you talked like an excavator. Incidentally, putting your muddy boots on *The Wall Street Journal* didn't hurt a bit."

How I Became a Labor Negotiator

Many years ago I had just started in the excavating business, and I was very inexperienced. We were a member of the Association of General Contractors of New Jersey, who negotiated contracts with labor unions. At a meeting I foolishly criticized a recently signed contract. The president of the association listened to my gripes and said I had a fine grasp of the situation and appointed me to the labor committee.

Several months later I was told to be at the Hotel Trent in Trenton, New Jersey, at nine o'clock in the morning to start negotiations with the heavy construction laborers' union. I met with several other contractors—they all employed many more laborers than my company did—and we discussed strategy. At ten o'clock the doors burst open and a dozen laborer union officials came in. They sat across the table from us and we greeted each other.

The laborer spokesman read a list of demands and the discussions began. Soon it seemed everyone was shouting and pounding the table with their fists. By eleven thirty the room was filled with smoke, and I wondered if I would get out alive!

I retreated to the men's room and went into a stall. Soon the head of the contractors and the head of the union came into the men's room. I lifted my feet off the floor as I had seen once in a movie, so nobody knew I was there.

"What do you guys need?" asked the contractor.

"Twenty-five cents per hour increase in pay," said the union official, "but I have a problem down in South Jersey. Nonunion competition is taking too much construction work from us, so we only want fifteen cents per hour there."

The contractor responded, "We can live with that. What about all those new labor work rules you are demanding?"

"Forget about them," said the union official, and they walked out of the men's room.

I returned to the meeting room thinking the negotiations were all over. They were not. There was still a lot of shouting and threatening. The two leaders I had heard in the men's room were shaking their fists at each other. At noontime the doors opened and waiters brought in food and drink. Things calmed down after a steak dinner, and we all went home.

Three weeks later I received a notice from the union. Wages would be going up twenty-five cents per hour in North Jersey and fifteen cents per hour in South Jersey.

I learned a lot:

1 - It only takes two people to make an agreement.

2 - It is good to let the troops have a chance to blow off steam and brag how tough they were when they get back to the union hall or at contractor meetings.

3 - Even unions are aware of competition.

Sanitary Sewers

The first sanitary sewers in Metuchen, New Jersey, used pipes made of a glazed tile material. The joints were "bell

and spigot"—which meant that one end of the pipe was flared to receive the next length of pipe. The joint was sealed with mortar, which did not bind well with tile, and the joints leaked. Since you can't get under the pipe to repair it when it is lying on the ground in the ditch, the joints at the bottom of the pipe would continuously leak. If the water table was high, ground water would seep in, causing more expense in treating more sewage water. Conversely, if the water table was low, raw sewage would ooze out of the pipe. This would encourage tree roots to grow into the pipe, eventually causing it to block up.

An improved pipe of longer lengths, made of cast iron, and which had caulked lead joints was used next. This resulted in much less chance of tree root infiltration. These pipes were especially used as laterals to the houses. Next came a tile pipe with bitumen joints that sealed very well. Another improvement was longer lengths of fiber cement pipe, with rubber gasket joints, resulting in very few leaks.

Today plumbers and site work contractors use plastic pipe with glued joints—installed with laser-beam precision. We liked this solution best.

All sanitary pipes eventually run into a manhole. Manholes were originally hand-laid and built of bricks. Later, manholes were stronger and made of precast concrete block. The manholes we most liked were those totally formed in a factory—precast concrete manholes which are the strongest and waterproof.

Years ago we had a sewer inspector named Mr. Reed. He was from Scotland and when he spoke he rolled his "R's" in a most delightful way. He would visit our sanitary sewer installation sites each day.

When the sewer was completed, he would have his final

inspection. He would instruct our foreman to block up the lowest outlet pipe. Then the inspection party would walk the length of the new sanitary line examining each manhole.

Since we had no television camera in those days, Mr. Reed had his own way of inspecting the buried underground pipe. At the last manhole Mr. Reed would reach into his pocket and produce a tennis ball. He dropped the tennis ball into the manhole and watched it roll down the pipe.

At the lowest manhole, Mr. Reed would instruct our foreman to go into the manhole and bring out the tennis ball. He explained to us that if there was a high spot in the pipe or a low spot in the pipe, the tennis ball would get stuck, as would the sewage eventually, and we would have failed our inspection. By rolling the ball the entire length of the new sanitary pipe, this would prove that the sewage would flow fine.

The foreman climbed out of the manhole and handed Mr. Reed the tennis ball and everyone was happy that we passed our final inspection. The foreman reached into his pocket and produced another tennis ball and said to Mr. Reed, "Just in case your tennis ball did not make it, I had a spare one." Everyone laughed.

Civic Duty

In 1962, Sonny had a fleet of dump trucks and he had a job with a contractor named Ray to haul dirt out of a borrow pit.

Ray was to be paid by measuring the pit before and after the government job was completed. Sonny stole many loads of dirt from the borrow pit during the job and sold it. About half of the dirt loaded at the pit never made it to the government jobsite. Ray knew this but liked it because he too would be paid for this stolen dirt by the government measurement method.

The government inspectors found out about the stealing but could not prove it. They took the money out of Ray's payments for other parts of the job.

Ray had to get even. He had another job on Interstate 287 in New Jersey that needed sand backfill against the bridge abutments. He bought the sand from a sandpit behind Middlesex County College and arranged for Sonny to truck the sand to the Interstate 287 jobsite. After the trucking was completed, Ray refused to pay Sonny.

The dispute ended up in a lawyer's office with Sonny at one end of a conference table and Ray at the other end. In between them were four lawyers.

Sonny presented his bill. Ray said it was correct but there were back charges. The state had rejected some of the sand.

Sonny got mad. He shouted, "It was your sand. You bought it. All I did was truck it." An argument started. Sonny got madder and madder. Then he got up, jumped forward, slid down the table, and started to choke Ray. The lawyers just sat there until Ray's face started to turn blue. Then collectively they pried Sonny lose.

The meeting adjourned.

Two week later Sonny drove onto Interstate 287, which in 1962 was just a dirt construction road. He pulled up to a foreman and asked, "Where is Ray?"

The foreman looked in the back seat of Sonny's car. There

were seated two very big, tough-looking men with their arms folded. They had on pork pie hats.

"Ray is down at the east end of the job," said the foreman. Actually he was at the west end. As Sonny pulled away, the foreman jumped in his pickup and drove down to warn Ray. His car was at the east end of the job so Ray walked out to U.S. Route 1 and hitchhiked home.

A week later I ran into Sonny and asked, "I heard you were down on 'two eighty seven' looking for Ray. What were you going to do?"

He told me his sad tale and finished by saying, "I was going to kill that _ _ _ _. But I've cooled down now."

"Sonny, killing him would have been a mortal sin," I said.

"No it wouldn't," he replied, "It would be my civic duty."

This story went throughout the construction industry in New Jersey. Many others had had bad experiences with Ray. Those who knew Ray agreed. It was Sonny's civic duty.

Depot Security

During the 1960's, there was a small group of suppliers whose main customers were heavy construction contractors. They held their high-pressure salesmen's annual picnic at the Ryland Inn on U.S. Route 22. The Ryland Inn had a large grove in the backyard that could hold several hundred people. Besides contractors, the suppliers also invited some government officials. The picnic was great fun, with lots of food, drink, and good conversation.

I was standing with a group of six men, some of whom I knew, when a stranger walked up and introduced himself as the person in charge of the Belle Meade GSA (General Service Administration) Depot in Hillsborough Township, New Jersey. During the Cold War, the United States Government's GSA used this depot to stockpile strategic materials in case of war. There were huge piles of various metals, including copper, zinc, lead, tin, antimony, mercury, and chromium. Inside the warehouses were huge quantities of raw rubber, kapok, and goose down. There were even steam heated storage tanks containing lard.

The contractors began to talk about the Depot, while the stranger remained silent. Some had worked construction jobs there and related their experiences. Someone said that the treasure stored there was worth more than the gold stored at Fort Knox. Someone else mentioned that there were a lot of narcotics stored there. Another contractor commented that he hoped that organized crime did not know about the narcotics. The conversation moved on to other subjects, and we all got back to eating.

The next morning two FBI (Federal Bureau of Investigation) agents walked into my office saying, "We have to talk!" They asked me all about the high-pressure salesmen's picnic, especially the conversation about Belle Meade Depot. I told them all that I knew. Then I asked, "What happened?"

After the conversation about the Depot, the guy in charge of the Depot called the FBI and said that organized crime was going to steal narcotics held by the government. The FBI and Federal Marshals were immediately dispatched to the Depot and found all the narcotics were safe.

However, there was only one guard at the gate, who had a gun but no bullets, and he did not know how to load the gun. That was the only security for the Depot.

I asked the FBI agent how I would show up on his official report. He answered, "Marty I'm putting you down as a concerned citizen. I can assure you that there is more than adequate security at the Depot now."

Selling Real Estate

Dorothy, a real estate agent, had an appointment to show a house for sale. She left the beauty parlor a little late because she decided to try a new hairdo. The hairdresser said that her new look would attract a lot of attention because of the stylish coiffure. Opening the door to the vacant house, Dorothy entered just as rain started pouring down.

The prospective buyers were due in a few minutes so she made a last minute check of the house, turning on the lights. Then she heard water running in the basement. Running down the stairs she found water coming in from a basement window. Dorothy went back upstairs and, peering out a window, saw the source of her problem. On the concrete patio, a drain was blocked up with leaves.

With no umbrella, she looked for something to cover her hair. In a trash can in a dark corner of the garage, she found a plastic bag and placed it over her hair. She kicked off her shoes, ran outside, unplugged the drain, and rushed back to the house.

The doorbell rang. Dorothy removed her hair covering, put her shoes back on, and greeted her customers. As she showed them around the house they kept staring at her hair. She smiled back, appreciating their interest. But they never stopped staring at her hair. She thought to herself that the hairdresser was right and her new coiffure was attracting a lot of attention.

After the customers left, she went back to the bathroom to turn out the light. She gasped as she looked in the mirror and saw her new hairdo. It was covered in pieces of broken potato chips.

Dorothy never saw those prospective real estate customers again. She went back to her old hairdo because the new coiffure had lost all its charm.

The Low Bid

Years ago when highway construction was going full blast, a New Jersey town advertised a job to prepare a site to build a new school. The job consisted of removing a hill of several thousand truckloads of material and then grading the site flat for the new school.

Sonny was a big trucking contractor who would love to get a job like this. However, he had lots of work and could not handle this new job, but he did not want his competitors to get it either. So on the day that the construction bids were going to be read, Sonny waited outside the public auditorium. As the last bid was opened and read, Sonny rushed into the room and said, "Sorry I am late, but here is my bid."

"You are too late," said the chairman, "All the bids have been opened and they are written on the blackboard."

Sonny looked at the blackboard and shouted, "I demand you open my bid, just for public information." Several of Sonny's friends strategically placed in the audience started shouting, and the chairman gave in. He opened Sonny's bid and read it aloud.

Sonny's bid was to pay the town for removing the earth! All the other bids were for the town to pay the contractors to remove the earth. There was a dead silence. The chairman asked Sonny why he was willing to pay the town for the dirt instead of charging the town to remove the dirt. Sonny replied, "I can sell this very good material to some road contractor." The motion was made and carried to rebid the project in two weeks.

At the next bid Sonny was in the front row with the bid envelope in his hand. The other bidders came into the room. Some carried two bid letters. Sonny watched the clock on the wall. At three minutes before the bid deadline Sonny put his bid envelope on the table. The other bidders came up and placed their bids on the table too. Those with two bid letters submitted the "If Sonny bids" bid letter.

As the bids were opened and read, it became obvious that the town was going to receive a lot of money for this hill of dirt. All the bids were to pay the town more money than Sonny's original bid.

The last bid to be opened was Sonny's. It was blank. Attached to it was a note saying, "It was my civic duty."

Fried Clams

Years ago, before cell phones, I was driving down U.S. Route 1 during the afternoon when a message came over the two-way radio from our office. A fellow contractor had called to ask if I could meet him at the local Howard Johnson's to discuss something very important. OK I replied.

Howard Johnson's was a chain of very nice restaurants that were clean and had a standard menu. As I drove along I thought of the twenty-eight different flavors of ice cream that Howard Johnson's featured. I scrolled down the list of my favorites, mentally tasting each one. Then fried clams, one of their specialties, popped into my head. Again I mentally tasted them with just a smidge of tartar sauce.

I arrived, entered the restaurant, and the manger motioned me to a secluded booth where the contractor sat. The waitress came to take our order. He asked for a strawberry sundae and I ordered a chocolate sundae with marshmallow sauce and a double order of fried clams.

We started talking. The waitress brought our order. She set the sundaes in front of us with the fried clams in the middle.

My friend took four or five fried clams and sprinkled them on his sundae. I didn't want to embarrass him so I sprinkled some fried clams on my sundae.

As we continued sprinkling the clams on the ice cream I noticed two waitresses and the manger staring at us. My friend said how good the clams and ice cream were and as we left he approached the manager saying, "You know, that was very good. You should put it on the menu."

I tried the clams and the ice cream a week later, but somehow it just wasn't the same.

The Great Gorge Playboy Club

In the early 1970's the Associated General Contractors of New Jersey held its yearly convention at the newly opened Great Gorge Playboy Club in Northern New Jersey. Our group leader went to the club two days early to make sure everything was in order. Over one hundred members and their families were expected. Even the Governor of New Jersey was coming to make a speech.

When our leader arrived, he was told he was to occupy the Hugh Hefner Suite with his wife. The suite was very impressive. A bedroom, a large entertainment room with a bar, and an oversized bathroom with two telephones, a separate multi-jet shower, and a large black marble bathtub.

Our leader went to see the manager while his wife unpacked. Two hotel maintenance men came to the room and told the wife they had to put a special sealer on the tub and not to use it until tomorrow, when the sealer would be dry.

She left to go shopping. Our leader returned. He filled the tub with nice warm water, took his current reading material, and settled into the tub for a nice long soak.

After a while the water was cooling so he tried to lean forward to run in a little hot water. He couldn't move! The hair on his back was stuck to the tub and so were his legs. Neither of the two telephones were within reach. All he could do was sit there and wait for his wife as the water cooled—and he had finished his reading.

After a wonderful hour of shopping in all the new shops, his wife returned. Our leader called her and explained his problem. She laughed. She tried to pull a leg loose with no success, so she called maintenance.

The two hotel maintenance men arrived. They laughed. They called the manager. He laughed.

The next hour was spent cutting the body hair loose using very sharp knives and razor blades. When our leader was freed, he was happy that there was no blood.

Everyone was sworn to secrecy. But I found out!

Plan Bulldozer

In the early 1970's during the term of Governor Cahill, the Associated General Contractors of New Jersey (mostly road builders) started a program to help government function in emergency situations. A current inventory of equipment, from air compressors, trucks, backhoes, bulldozers to large cranes, was maintained. Another list of the individuals who could both mobilize and transport equipment and supply skilled operators and supervision was compiled. This project was called "Plan Bulldozer."

A large meeting of contractors, the press, and interested parties was arranged. As chairman I was to give a speech explaining Plan Bulldozer. The president of the Contractor's Association would then present a copy of the plan to the Governor of New Jersey. Just before the presentation, an aide to the governor asked me to explain the plan. I gave him a copy of my speech, which explained it all.

Soon I was sitting on the stage in front of a big crowd. The Governor was introduced to say a few words. As I sat there, I realized he was giving my speech!

Then they called on me. I did not feel too good. I got up to the podium and said, "Ladies and gentlemen, I hope you all paid close attention to Governor Cahill. He literally took the words right out of my mouth! He just gave my speech, and did a much better job than I could." I sat down to riotous laughter and then applause.

It all worked out OK, and everyone would remember Plan Bulldozer.

During a summer drought, New York had excess water and New Jersey had a shortage. The solution was to install a temporary water line across the George Washington Bridge. Over twenty low bed trailers were mobilized to haul ductile iron pipe from South Jersey to the bridge. In just two days, the lengths of pipe were strung out, connected together, hooked up to the New York City water supply, and New Jersey had the water it needed.

This program went nationwide and eventually was taken over by the Federal Government and is now called FEMA (Federal Emergency Management Agency). Of course the

Federal Government can do a better job than a bunch of (New Jersey) contractors who essentially do this type of work all the time. Just ask the people of New Orleans.

A Day at the Races

In the 1970's our excavating company, Arnolt Bros, Inc., was hired to rebuild the Freehold Raceway. Located in Freehold, New Jersey, this track is still used today for horse races. The entire track had to be torn up, lengthened, leveled from end to end, and then upgraded. We worked very hard and finished the job early.

A few days before the grand reopening of the race track, there was a very heavy rainstorm. Suddenly, at the third turn of the race track, a large hole appeared. It was twenty feet deep, fifteen feet in diameter, and shaped like a mason jar. A dozen experienced people stared curiously into the hole. What happened to all the dirt? Races were scheduled to start in four days.

Someone noticed two tennis balls floating at the bottom of the hole. "That is storm water," he said, "There are always balls floating on top of storm water." The old plans from the original construction of the track were found and carefully examined. The plans showed the location of a storm water pipe at the third turn in the track. It was a twenty-four-inch pipe that was laid on a curve—and that was a construction no-no. A joint of that pipe had opened up, which created an underground whirlpool that caused the dirt to wash down the storm drain.

We went to work immediately. The offending storm line was intercepted and a new storm sewer line was installed. Tons of rock was trucked in to fill up the hole. A reinforced concrete slab was poured over the hole—at four feet below the surface of the track. The track surface layers were rebuilt eliminating all traces of the hole. All this work was accomplished in two days.

On opening day the track personnel director asked us to supply four men to help with the parking. Before the races were over, a woman came up to the men and said she had to leave early for an emergency, and unfortunately she forgot where she parked her car. The car was brand new and she could not remember the make of the car or the color. All she knew was that her husband complained that the new car had a dented rear hubcap.

Four men fanned out to search the full parking lot for a new car with a dented rear hubcap. After fifteen minutes of searching one of the men brought the lady to a car that matched her description. She was so happy that we had found her car. On top of her car was a red canoe!

The Wheelbarrow

The Metuchen Savings Bank started in 1897 as the Metuchen Building and Loan Association. The original building and loan idea was for a group of people to pool their savings together. Each person made a regular monthly contribution to the pool, and when enough money was accumulated to build or purchase a home, one member would be selected (sometimes by lot) and they would receive a mortgage loan from the association.

In Metuchen's case it started with investment shares and installment shares. The money raised was used to purchase a tract of land known as "Woodwild in the Village of Metuchen, New Jersey." It was the area that was roughly east of Main Street and north of Middlesex Avenue. The land was then sold off as building lots.

The Metuchen Building and Loan chugged along through World War I, the Great Depression, and World War II. In 1960 it became Metuchen Savings and Loan with Federal Deposit Insurance. The bank moved to 429 Main Street and started to grow.

One afternoon, I was approached by a bank examiner who was asking me about the different bank officers. "You have Mr. S. as treasurer. Why is he your treasurer and how old is he?" he growled at me.

In an honest reply I said, "I don't know how old he is. Maybe sixty or seventy I guess. He is retired and has time to be around the bank to sign large checks."

I had the feeling that the bank examiner did not like old folks in positions of authority. He then sneered at me asking, "Is there any other reason?"

"Yes," I replied, "He has a wheelbarrow."

Now the bank examiner was aghast. "What does a wheelbarrow have to do with running a bank?" was his next question.

I explained, "We have the only public coin counter in town. Once or twice a week, we take our coins across the street to the National Bank for the armored car to pick them up. There are a lot of coins and they are heavy, so we need a wheelbarrow."

Now the bank examiner looked at me as if I was a nut. Just

at that moment the back door opened, and in walked a police officer followed by Mr. S. with his wheelbarrow.

Every once in a while you have to be lucky, and Mr. S. was in his eighties.

Chickens and Eggs

Years ago, one of my cousins represented a chemical company to a farmer's cooperative. He called on one cooperative that ran a large egg producing unit. It was a large building that contained thousands of chickens, each in its own cage. There were long rows of them on several floors.

Each chicken's vitamin enriched food was automatically dispensed to each cage. When an egg was laid, it rolled through a counter, then onto a conveyer belt that took the eggs to the processing room. There they were cleaned, inspected, and graded automatically. Then, the last step was the packing machine that put the eggs into boxes and slid them onto a table to be hand packed into crates.

As my cousin walked into the building, there was bedlam. The packing machine had broken down and eight people were shoulder to shoulder putting the eggs into boxes. It was obvious that the chickens were getting ahead of the packers. The owner called my cousin over and asked him to take his place while he telephoned for more help. Eggs had begun dropping to the floor, making footing a little slippery.

The mechanic reported that he needed parts and they would not arrive until the next morning. Two more packers came in to help, one with his ten-year-old son.

The boy watched the scene with amazement. Then he went to the owner, tugged on his sleeve and asked, "Why don't you turn off the lights?"

The lights in the chicken area were turned off. In a few minutes, the flow of eggs slowed to a trickle.

The owner shook the boy's hand and said, "When you turn sixteen years old, come here. You will have a job."

Trade Associations

I spent over forty years as a contractor in the excavating business. It may look like dirt to you, but it was bread and butter to me.

Our company was a member of the AGC (Associated General Contractors) of New Jersey. The members of this group built most of the Garden State Parkway, New Jersey Turnpike, and Interstate Highway System. They also built sewage treatment plants, airports, and reservoirs. These were giants of the industry with permanent staffs, hundreds of employees, and large fleets of heavy equipment. Compared to them, I was strictly small time. But they treated me very well and made me feel like one of the gang. They even put me on committees. When I was put on the labor committee to help negotiate union contracts, it was truly an educational experience.

The local chapter was a part of the National AGC, which also had its advantages. When OSHA (Occupational Health and Safety Administration) came into effect, one of the regulations prohibited ice in drinking water. No one could explain why. It was turned over to the National AGC.

What followed was hard to believe. Before mechanical refrigeration, ice was harvested during the winter from ponds and lakes. It was stored in large insulated buildings for summer use. The ice was harvested using horse-drawn "sleds" with teeth on the runners to score the ice before it was chopped into blocks to be packed in the ice house. Therefore, the ice had varying amounts of horse manure in it. That was the reason for the regulation. Perhaps you have seen old pitchers with two compartments—one for the ice and one for the beverage.

It took the National AGC over a year to get the regulation removed to allow us to put ice in drinking water. Apparently it is very easy to get a new regulation implemented but almost impossible to get an outdated one removed.

Every business should investigate to see if there is a trade association for their industry, and, if one exists, they should join. All businesses should join their local Chamber of Commerce.

I was often asked what it was like working with the giants of the construction industry, and I explained it this way: It is like being a mouse with a herd of elephants. Be careful not to get stepped on and when everyone marches across a bridge, you, as the mouse, turn around and say, "Boy, we sure shook the heck out of that bridge!"

Pennies

Years ago the value of the United States dollar was slipping and the price of copper was rising. A friend of mine, R. Bruce McDowell, was in the silver business. He had an office on the second floor over the Commonwealth Bank at 407 Main Street in Metuchen, New Jersey. He would buy and sell silver tableware and other things made of silver. Most of it was sold for scrap.

Bruce decided that he would start accumulating pennies to cash in when the price of copper rose. He visited all the local banks and bought all the five-thousand-penny bags he could find.

I visited him one day and found a pile of penny bags almost two feet high and ten feet long right in the center of the room. I warned him that the floor was overloaded. A few more bags and everything would come crashing down to the first floor, right on top of the desk of the bank president, Mr. J. Arthur Applegate.

We quickly moved the bags over to the side walls. Time went on and more and more penny bags were brought into his office.

Then the price of copper fell. Some people began mocking his business ability and soon it got to be quite a joke. My friend blithely kept buying pennies.

Then the Christmas shopping season came and suddenly there was a shortage of pennies. The banks knew where they were and bought the pennies back at a ten to twenty percent mark-up.

The armored car crews complained bitterly that they had to carry the bags of pennies down from the second floor. Who would ever imagine that someone could corner the penny market!

Where's Harry?

In 1994, when Metuchen Savings Bank built their new Victorian office building on Pearl Street, it became necessary to connect the drive-up facility on Pearl Street with the bank on Main Street. One day I was in a meeting with the engineers who designed the drive-up facility.

The connection between the two buildings would be in a ditch. As a ditch digger, I could handle that. When the discussion of the underground connection got under way, we realized that the pneumatic tube with the traveling torpedo would have to go in many different directions. This requirement was causing much difficulty. I sensed that the engineers were having trouble.

I said, "Why can't we get that gray-haired guy to come and take a look at all of this?"

"You mean Harry?" they asked.

"Yes, Harry," I replied.

The next day Harry showed up. In a few minutes all the problems were solved. As we left the meeting one of the engineers asked, "How did you know about Harry?"

I answered, "There is always a Harry. You just have to find him."

The *Delta Queen*

We took a Civil War sightseeing cruise on the stern wheel steamboat the *Delta Queen*. There was a Civil War style band with "over the shoulder" instruments to welcome us. An "over the shoulder" band had instruments with the bell end facing to the rear so that the troops marching behind could hear the music. Each day we had lectures and field trips to historic sites.

I first traveled on the *Delta Queen* during World War II. In San Francisco Bay, the *Delta Queen* and the *Delta King* were used to ferry Army, Navy, and Marine personnel about the harbor. My trip was from Treasure Island (the site of the 1939 World's Fair) to Pier No. 7, San Francisco, California, where we embarked upon the troop transport, the USS *General* M. B. *Stewart* (AP-140), which was heading to the Western Pacific. Over three thousand Naval personnel traveled on the paddle wheelers for the numerous short trips, packed in and mostly standing or sitting on their sea rolls.

The Civil War cruise was very active and interesting. The principal speaker was a professor from the University of Virginia. When he spoke of the "enemy," he meant the "**&¢%$** Yankees."

At the final lecture he asked if there were any questions. My hand shot up. I asked, "Who *really* won the Civil War?" Very sadly he said the North won. I replied by saying, "No, the South *really* won." As a good professor he asked, "What is your reasoning for that idea?"

"It is very simple," I replied, "The Boston Navy Yard is closed, and so are the Brooklyn Navy Yard and the Philadelphia Navy Yard as well. On the east coast, the main working Navy Yard is in Norfolk, Virginia. Most of the space programs are in Confederate States. So are most of the military training facilities. You can also add the Raritan Arsenal and Fort Monmouth in New Jersey and Governor's Island in New York Harbor to the list of the facilities that have all been closed. Of every dollar that New Jersey taxpayers send to Washington, only sixty-five cents comes back. A lot of the thirty-five cents goes to the Confederacy. Now, you tell me who won."

The Celotex Factory

On Middlesex Avenue in Metuchen, New Jersey, along the Greenway that once was the Lehigh Valley Railroad tracks, was the factory of the Celotex Company. (Later this site would become the location of the Oakite Factory.) Celotex was an insulating wall board made from the waste of sugar cane. We didn't know about recycling in those days; many waste items were simply reused for another purpose. Some Celotex was sold as plain sheets, while others were covered with a hard layer of asbestos cement board.

Previously this site had been used as a tile factory. Before that, the site was a storage area for World War I war materials. All of this history made the dump site behind the factory a wonderful playground for young boys during the Great Depression. There were two metal lifeboats, only slightly broken. We played that we were pirates. There were all sorts of tile, including wall tiles of numerous colors and small size floor tiles. We always brought some home to triumphantly show our moms: "Look what I found!"

Then there were the fires. The dump was burned every week to keep the size of the garbage down. So we had to be real careful some days.

Since the railroad tracks were right next to where we were playing, we would watch the long coal cars rumble past as we waved to the engineer. He always waved back. The railroad used a small camelback switch engine to bring freight cars up to the factory and to move loaded cars out. This was so interesting to watch, that to this day I think we really had it better than the kids today with television and computers. All of this activity was in living color, with smells, and in three dimensions.

Oakite came to Metuchen after Celotex moved to Perth Amboy. Oakite employed about one hundred and fifty people, paid taxes, and manufactured many different cleaning products.

This leads to a sad story about our state government at work. In 1988 Oakite was bought by the Carlyle Group. A short time after they bought the company, a delivery of nitric acid was made to the Oakite factory in Metuchen. Through a foul up in the paperwork, twice as much nitric acid as was needed was ordered and delivered, which caused the holding tank to spill over. The spill was contained in a concrete lined area. The Oakite employees neutralized the acid and cleaned it up. They promptly notified six different federal and state government agencies of the accident. Unfortunately, there was a seventh state government agency (that they did not know about) that was late in being notified.

Because of this notification failure, Oakite was fined twenty thousand dollars by the state government of New Jersey. This incident happened just as the Carlyle Group was deciding which of the four Oakite factories in the United States to close. Oakite, with a long history in chemical manufacturing, understood the accident and how it happened, and accepted that. What they could not understand was New Jersey's government punishing them, when nobody was hurt, there was no harm to the environment, and their own employees cleaned up everything.

The Carlyle Group decided to keep the factories in Los Angeles, Detroit, and Houston open, and to close down the factory in Metuchen. One of the largest employers Metuchen ever had left town and gone forever were many high-paying union jobs for Metuchen and for New Jersey.

I Won't Marry Her

I served as a management trustee on a union pension and wel-fare (health) plan fund. I learned a lot. Mostly trustees end up dealing with multitudes of problems.

The wife of one of our retired members applied for open heart surgery. Part of the application was to furnish a copy of the marriage certificate. We were informed they could not find the certificate.

The fund employee asked where they were married. The answer was, "Elkton, Maryland." During the 1940's you could go to Elkton, get a marriage license and be married instantly. Most other states required a waiting period, which resulted in hundreds of thousands of anxious couples being married in Elkton. The fund contacted Elkton and no record was found of the member's marriage.

This couple was in their seventies with five grown children and fourteen grandchildren. I asked a question, "If a retired member marries a twenty-one-year-old young lady would she be covered?" The answer was, "Yes."

A letter was sent to the member suggesting he go to a local justice of the peace and marry his wife again. This would unclog the paperwork for the operation.

A short time later a letter was received from the member stating, "I am not going to do it!"

At the next trustee meeting we were aghast at the reply. "What happened?" was asked. "She must have burned the toast," was the answer.

Incidentally, she lived for many years, without the heart operation.

Shoes

At my first New York Boat Show working as a salesman, I was in the sailboat section, in the top of the line Catalina Yacht, which cost several hundred thousand dollars.

I was assigned to sit in the cockpit, greet people who boarded, and answer questions. The main salesman, Bob (Robert) Dolan, was in the cabin below.

As my instructor, Bob explained that I had to identify the most likely buyers. Most of the people were just looking, and most said so. I was told to observe how people were dressed, particularly their shoes.

If the shoes they wore were "Top-Siders" you knew they were boat people. If the companion lady had high heels and was the wife—there was a slight hope. If she wasn't the wife—there was no hope.

One afternoon a well dressed husband and wife came aboard. I looked at their feet. Both had old beat-up Top-Siders on with brand new soles. My instructions hadn't covered this.

The wife sat in the cockpit with me while the husband went below. "You noticed my Top-Siders," she said. "I just got them re-soled for the second time. When they are broken in they are so comfortable."

She asked questions about the sailboat, very intelligent questions. I asked where she would be sailing and she replied, "The Hudson River and New York Harbor."

I took a swig of my Pepsi-Cola and asked, "Are you thinking of buying this boat?"

"Yes," she replied, "My husband is discussing certain layout changes we want."

Soon the husband and Bob Dolan, the main salesman, came up and sat in the cockpit. The main salesman had the order form filled out. He handed a copy to the husband who studied it then said it was OK.

Bob told them it would require a twenty percent down payment because of the changes. The husband took out his checkbook and wrote the check.

"Do you want to finance the balance?" asked Bob.

"No, I'll have a certified check for you on delivery," answered the husband.

If you ever see re-soled Top-Siders, remember this story.

Uncle Gus

A few years ago I was a sailboat salesman at the annual New York Boat Show at the Jacob K. Javits Convention Center in New York City. As a salesman you try to point out the advantages of the boat you are selling. However there are also disadvantages that sooner or later have to be discussed. Sailboat design is all about compromises. How do the advantages fit the potential customer?

At some point you sense the sale is close. How do you close the sale? I told the story of my Uncle Gus, Gustav Mattson.

My Uncle Gus apprenticed as a machinist when he was in

his mid-teens. It was a tough school but he learned well. He got a job at the Raritan Copper Works in Perth Amboy, New Jersey. Eventually he became the superintendent of the machine shop.

All during the Great Depression he had a well-paid full time job. When my family went to visit him the conversation was always about boats. The boat he wanted, where he would keep it, and where he would sail it. He studied all the yachting magazines. He even built a steam engine to power it. He could well afford to buy the boat, but he never did. He had years of dreams, but died having never owned a sailboat.

This story usually got results. One customer came back several times, and, hearing of Uncle Gus, he finally decided to buy the boat. While he was doing the paperwork with the main salesmen his wife came up to me. She shook my hand and told me her husband had wanted a boat for years. "Thank you. Thank you!" she said.

I replied, "Don't thank me. Thank Uncle Gus."

The Model

When I was in my sixties, I was helping my daughter Nancy sell sailboats at the New York Boat Show at the Jacob K. Javits Convention Center in New York City. The boat show took up the entire main floor. In the large ground floor was the International Fashion Boutique Show, where manufacturers displayed and sold their merchandise to shop and store owners.

These shows represented two very diverse cultures. A cafeteria in the lower level was shared by both shows.

At lunchtime, I took my tray to an empty table where I could face the people coming with their full trays. I spread *The Wall Street Journal* on the table and started to eat and read. Suddenly the room became quiet. I looked up and smiled as I saw a very beautiful young lady coming toward me. She came to my table and asked if she could sit down.

Yes! She sat down, pulled out a side chair and put her foot on it. She displayed a very high heel shoe with a pointy toe as she began massaging her foot. "These shoes are killing me," she said, "They are the newest fashion. How do you like the leg?"

"Very nice," I replied as she switched legs and began massaging the other foot.

Then she finished massaging, sat back in her chair, and threw her shoulders back. I could not help looking at the next display.

"Are they new?" I inquired.

"Yes, six months ago."

"How much did they cost?"

"Ten thousand dollars."

"Apiece or the pair?"

"The pair."

"Did it hurt?"

"Only a few days."

"Has it changed your life?"

"It certainly has. I was usually booked up modeling for a week or two. Now I'm booked over eight months ahead and my rate has tripled. That is why I want to talk to you. I figure I have five to ten years of this. I'll earn a lot of money and I want to invest it for my old age."

I talked of dividend paying stocks, utilities, and dividend re-investment plans. She took notes. She thanked me and walked away.

I was crestfallen. I thought she chose my table because of my winning smile, but realized it wasn't me; it was *The Wall Street Journal* that attracted her. However, that was one smart lady.

Priorities

Years ago Sam Owen called me and said that PSE&G (Public Service Electric & Gas) was coming before the Metuchen, New Jersey, Planning Board with a proposal to extend the column supports for the electrical system on the old Pennsylvania Railroad line (the main lines for New Jersey Transit and Amtrak today). The extension work would be about twenty feet of new structural steel atop approximately sixty feet of old rusted steel. The purpose was to support new electrical power transmission lines. He asked if I had any comments.

I had been worrying about the rusting away of the entire steel support system. The upper wires carry one hundred and thirty-two thousand volts. A steel column can only rust so much, and then something fails, causing the trains to stop, and permanent repairs would be extremely expensive and a night-mare to fix.

I told this to Sam and suggested that they should be required to paint the columns. My thought was to paint the entire eighty-foot column. Sam thought that was a good idea.

PSE&G installed the extension columns and painted the upper twenty feet but never painted the old rusty bottom portion of the columns. To this day they continue to rust away.

It is strange that our society has the money to build a new Giants Stadium (twice!), a structure used to capacity twenty to twenty-five times a year for approximately five hours each time.

But our society can't find the money to maintain a railroad that carries thousands of passengers to work each day.

Congress

M any people seem unhappy with the United States Congress. Congress passes numerous laws, some with unintended consequences. There is a law that in a few years incandescent light bulbs will no longer be sold. They must be replaced with other more efficient lights. Congress thinks the American people are too dumb to save on electricity so they must do it for us. Even though incandescent bulbs use more power, there are still many important uses for them. Many fixtures will need to be replaced because of the shape of the new bulbs. Imagine Imagine American citizens going to Mexico to buy incandescent light bulbs!

Something to think about: When a person is elected to Congress, the first thing they do is to start on their re-election.

It takes a lot of time to raise money because an election campaign is very expensive.

Who is running the country? The correct answer is the congressional staffs. They are mostly young people, usually fresh out of college. They turn out the one-thousand or two-thousand-page bills that the congressmen who vote on them do not have enough time to read.

We need a new regulation; no one can serve on a congressional staff unless they are at least fifty years old and have met a payroll. They need to have life experience.

Reporters once asked a businessman the secret of his success. "Good decisions," he answered. "How do you make good decisions?" was the next question. "Experience," he said. "How did you get experience?" With a thoughtful smile, he replied, "Bad decisions."

Is it good for the United States to have our congressional staffs getting experience by making so many bad decisions?

Big Bus, Little Bus

Have you ever noticed the large buses that roam through our town of Metuchen, New Jersey? At the railroad station they pick up workers and students to take them to their destinations. All of these bus and train passengers are not paying the full price of their tickets. People who buy gasoline and diesel fuel pay a fuel tax that subsidizes mass transit rider tickets by fifty percent or more. The theory behind this redirecting of motor vehicle taxes away from road construction or repair is that the tax subsidy for mass transit riders reduces the number of drivers on the road, which would be a benefit to drivers paying the tax.

About a year ago the public transportation buses put up large advertising signs that do not allow you to see the passengers. Most of the time the number of passengers was a small number compared to the capacity of the bus. My suspicion is that the advertising signs bring in revenue and hide the fact that the big buses are underutilized.

I wonder why the transit company doesn't have any smaller buses in their fleet. These smaller buses could carry fewer people and save money by using less fuel and creating less air pollution. It would help the air quality in town if these diesel buses, which probably use imported oil, could be converted to natural gas, which the United States has a hundred year supply of and burns cleaner. Smaller buses would also ease congestion as they go around corners quicker and easier.

In the 1920's, local public transportation was by trolleys. Most local trolley companies had their own power plants to make electricity to power the trolleys. In Metuchen the local power plant was by the old Lehigh Valley Railroad crossing on Durham Avenue (today it is the Middlesex County Greenway). The trolley companies sold some of their electric power to residences. When the trolley on Main Street climbed the hill at the Pennsylvania Railroad Bridge, the lights in town would dim.

Eventually Public Service Electric & Gas bought out the trolley companies and went strictly into the power business as buses replaced trolleys because they could travel places trolleys could not go.

Today if the operators of the big buses had rider counts by route and time, they could devise a schedule of where smaller buses could be used. This little bit of thinking and management could save money, cut air pollution, and increase traffic mobility.

This is just my observation. But I am optimistic that a higher authority has already examined this and that soon we will see both the Big Bus and Little Bus—all fueled by natural gas.

The Advantage of a Small Town

It was noontime the day before Christmas and there was a call for the president of the bank. It was from a former resident of Metuchen, New Jersey, who had left town many years ago. The lady was ninety-six years old and living in Missouri.

She asked if she could have help putting two wreaths on her father's and mother's grave. She also said her father had been a director of the Metuchen Building and Loan Association many years ago.

She said that in the past Jack Boeddinghaus the florist or Marty Jessen had taken care of it. The president tried to contact Jack or Marty, but to no avail.

The bank president then called the hardware store, ordered the wreaths, and asked that they be delivered to the cemetery caretaker.

Next a call was made to the cemetery and a discussion ensued about the location of the graves. The caretaker was not sure of the location but he said he would try to find them.

Later, just at closing time, a call from the cemetery—mission accomplished! Then a call was made to the ninety-six-year-old daughter, telling of the success and making one old lady happy for Christmas.

Running a Meeting

I received a call from the chairman of the Delaware and Raritan Canal Commission telling me that he would not be at the next meeting and I would have to run the meeting as vice-chairman. He warned me that one item on the agenda was to be protested by the leader of an environmental group that was politically connected. I was to be very polite and diplomatic.

At the meeting the item was presented. A volunteer fire company, which had a one-hundred-foot radio tower at their firehouse, wanted to have their antenna replaced with a one-hundred-twenty-foot tower. This was to have their antenna at the top give them much better coverage. The new tower would also hold two cell phone arrays that would pay them substantial rent, permitting them to buy more up-to-date fire equipment.

When the lady objector stood up she pointed out that the present tower was an eyesore sticking up above the surrounding trees. The new tower would be a more intrusive eyesore with the additional height and the horrible cell phone arrays;

not just one array—but two and possibly a third.

At that point the cell phone representative said it was customary for various cell phone companies to concentrate locations on one tower to cut down on the total number of towers required.

The objector brought up more points. She started to repeat things and I started to worry. This should have been a slam dunk for the firemen, but her arguments were wearing us all down.

Then it happened. Her pocketbook started to ring!

She snatched up her pocketbook, but had trouble getting it opened. The ringing was very persistent. Finally, she got the phone out, answered it, and said, "Hello, I'll call you back."

I said, "Madam, you have made your point. Thank you very much."

The replacement tower was approved. I was accused of having someone call her. I didn't; it was her daughter.

Timing in life can be everything.

Pension Plans

The funding of defined benefit pension plans is complicated. To understand you should imagine a large water tank, the water being money.

A large pipe empties into the tank, bringing in employer contributions. In some plans, employees make contributions to the pension fund, so there would be another input pipe that empties their contributions into the tank.

The money in the tank is invested, bringing in another input pipe with a stream of investment income (interest, dividends, etc.). Other outside factors affect the water in the tank. When it rains (the stock market goes up), the amount of water in the tank increases. Sometimes the water leaks out (the stock market goes down), and the amount of money in the tank decreases.

At the bottom of the tank is an output pipe that pays benefits to the retired. A person called an *actuary* does the computations on how much water you need in the tank. He looks years ahead, estimating when employees will retire, estimating how long they will live, estimating their final pay, and, in some cases, estimating the same longevity information about their spouses. The sum of all his estimates tells us how much water there needs to be in the tank for the plan to be fully funded.

There is an assumption of how much income will come from investments. If investment income goes down, the volume of water in that input pipe decreases. If employment is reduced, the employer and employee (either or both depending upon the pension plan) contribution pipes slow down, and less water comes in.

If the investment income rate of return goes from eight percent to three percent, then the employer contribution must be increased. If the volume of the total water decreases (leaks), the contributions have to be increased. If the amount of pension paid out to retirees increases, then more water is required.

To figure the amount of water needed, the actuary assumes a rate of interest for a long period of time. Thus, if the assumed rate of eight percent equates to the plan being fully funded, lowering the assumed rate to six percent would cause the plan to be severely underfunded.

There is a fee for handling the investments; usually around one percent. This fee is charged even if the investments lose value (leak). If the earned investment income is eight percent, after the fee is charged the return is reduced to seven percent. If the investment income is three percent, the fee reduces the volume of investment water added to the tank to two percent.

There is a story of a Board of Directors meeting of a large corporation. The question before the board was: "How much is two plus two?"

They asked the accountant and he answered, "Four."

They asked the lawyer. His reply was, "Someplace between three and five. If we get the right judge, I could probably get you four and a half."

Then they asked the actuary. He got up, locked the doors, drew the window drapes closed, and asked, "How much do you want it to be?"

Cracker Boxes

Have you ever noticed that cracker boxes are not filled up? I know that crackers are sold by weight, but why the bigger box? Won't the oversized box give the crackers room to bounce around? The amount of extra box probably doesn't represent too many trees, but the right size box would make the shipping case smaller, which would allow a truck to carry more crackers. Maybe the bigger box makes the customer think they are getting more crackers.

Perhaps someone should start a new cracker company called "The Full Box Cracker Company." They could advertise "Our crackers ride in a full box, snuggled together to protect each other from shock. Our shipping costs are less and trees are saved by our frugality."

I am sure that the "Almost Full" cracker companies have all thought of this, but the resulting design of their boxes still give the public less for their money.

Perhaps "Almost Full" should think about Luke 6:38

"Give, and it will be given to you;
good measure, pressed down, shaken together,
running over, they will pour into your lap.
For by your standard of measure
it will be measured to you in return."

CHAPTER 9

Family Life

Taking Care of Baby

My wife Barbara was to spend the evening with the "High School Girls" and I was to babysit. She had written instructions for me. I picked up the first instruction sheet which explained how to feed the baby, and read as follows:

> Heat bottle of milk in pan of water.
>
> Shake a drop of milk onto inside of elbow.
>
> If it feels neither hot nor cold, the temperature is right.
>
> Hold baby on lap and feed.
>
> After feeding, put towel over shoulder and lean baby over to get a burp. Sometimes burps are liquid, that is the reason for the towel.
>
> Put baby back in crib. If baby smiles, it does not mean baby is glad to see you. It means there is more gas. Burp again.

The second instruction sheet for changing diapers read:

> When baby's diaper must be changed, first put a clean diaper on table. Imagine the diaper is a baseball field. Pick up second base and fold it onto home plate.
>
> Now pick up baby, take off soiled diaper, wipe bottom clean, and place baby on baseball field with baby's back on pitcher's mound.
>
> Fold home plate/second base over baby's belly. Then take first base and third base and safety pin together with home plate/second base.

I followed the instructions and they worked very well. Being married to a New York Yankees fan has hidden benefits.

However, after the diapering was completed, a home run was hit and the whole process had to be repeated again.

The Medicine Man

Many moons ago my young son and I were in the YMCA (Young Men's Christian Association) group called Indian Guides. By default I was given the American Indian leadership position of Medicine Man.

Harry Williams, YMCA secretary, asked me to visit a new tribe in Edison, New Jersey, and give them information and ideas for Indian Guide activities.

I put on my costume: moccasins, fringed shirt, and leggings. Then I placed my medicine pole and a large horned headdress in the car and drove out to Edison.

Before entering the house where the Guides were meeting, I put war paint on my face and then my large horned headdress on my head.

The front door of the house was open with a closed screen door. Through the screen door I could hear voices inside. I opened the screen door and with medicine pole in hand, jumped into the living room and shouted, "HOW!"

There were many women in the room and they all started screaming. I was in the wrong house! Then (it is hard to imagine with my great costume) somebody recognized me and everybody laughed. These were the wives and mothers of the tribe meeting next door.

Lesson one: Check the address
Lesson two: Knock before entering
Lesson three: Don't embellish the plan too much

The Reading Ramble

Back in the days when railroads were changing from steam engines to diesel engines (the 1960's), we went on an all-day trip with steam engine enthusiasts. Some of my family was worried that not too many people would go. We arrived at Bound Brook, New Jersey, to board the steam train and were amazed to see about two thousand people ready to ride with us.

The large 4-6-4 steam engine was at the head of a long string of passenger cars. 4-6-4 represents the steam engine wheel arrangement of four leading wheels on two axles, six powered and coupled driving wheels on three axles, and four trailing wheels on two axles. The local fire department was busy filling the tender with water, which was also heaped with anthracite (hard) coal. This was a class operation.

We boarded the train and sat in our seats. Across the aisle, by an open window, sat an older man wearing an engineer's hat and goggles. He fastened a padded arm rest on the sill and leaned out the window and shouted, "OK, let's get started."

"All aboard!" shouted the conductor. With a cloud of steam and a blast of the whistle, the train lurched ahead. We were on our way to Macungie, Pennsylvania. The train had a baggage car behind the engine, with safety bars across the doors. Steam engine enthusiasts came with tape recorders to tape the powerful sound of the steam engine. On the curves, cameras were held out the windows to capture the sight of the beautiful engine.

Soon the floor of the baggage car was gritty with cinders that blew in through the doors. Later, children would gather up the cinders into paper cups for souvenirs. In the car behind the baggage car was a doctor who was set up to take cinders out of people's eyes. He was busy but no one seemed concerned.

After three hours the train stopped on a curve. Many people piled off the train to take pictures. The train backed up about a mile, and then came charging ahead as it passed the cameras, putting out big clouds of black smoke and white steam. Then the train backed up and the picture takers climbed back aboard.

The train stopped at Macungie where they filled the tender up with water. A parade with lots of automobiles approached. We got off the train, into the cars, and the local high school band played as we made our way to a park with a stage. One half of the passengers went to eat a fried chicken dinner, while the other half watched the stage show put on by the townspeople. Then the passengers switched places.

When we finished, another parade took us back to the train and it was "All aboard!" again. The trip back to New Jersey seemed much shorter. Maybe it had something to do with the fried chicken, dumplings, and large selection of pies that made dozing very easy.

The Reading Railroad gave us memories and lots of pictures to mark the passing of the age of steam.

I Did Something Bad

Many years ago I had gone to bed early to get a good night's rest as I had to get up early for a very important meeting. I was sound asleep when the telephone rang.

Out of a deep sleep I answered the phone. A voice asked, "Is this Korvettes?" I answered, "Yes." That "Yes" started me on the road to deceit.

Started in New York City in 1948, E. J. Korvettes was one of the first chains of discount department stores, similar to today's "Target." The name E. J. Korvettes was coined as a combination of the founder's initials (Eugene and Joe) and a re-spelling of the naval term Corvette. A corvette is a small, maneuverable, lightly armed warship often used to escort convoys.

The caller explained he had purchased a twenty-foot diameter above ground swimming pool and with the help of neighbors was filling it with four hoses. I asked if he had the pool leveled up. He said he did but asked, "How do we get in the pool?" "You need a ladder," I replied, and then I asked, "What color is the pool?" "It's blue," was the answer.

I was getting warmed up so I stepped on the side of evil by saying, "You know we close at nine o'clock in the evening. A blue pool takes a red ladder. We only have one left. If you come over to Korvettes, go around to the back door, pound on it good, I'll give you the ladder."

My wife heard all of this and after I hung up she said, "Marty that was a terrible thing you did."

I said, "He knew the store was closed. He dialed the wrong number and woke me up. A terrible thing to do would be to call the Woodbridge Police Department and tell them someone is trying to break into the rear of Korvettes!"

Christmas Parades

Years ago we had Christmas Parades in Metuchen, New Jersey. The local service clubs and other organizations had floats or marching units. Prizes were given for the best participants.

In the early 1960's, the Metuchen Rotary Club had the float with Miss Merry Christmas and her court. The Miss Merry Christmas contest was supported by Morris Stores and they provided very nice shawls for each contestant to wear on the float. The contest generated much publicity.

Some people thought this gave the Rotary Club an unfair advantage in the prize competition because they always had a sure winner. So the Metuchen Chamber of Commerce took over the Miss Merry Christmas float.

The Rotary Club had to come up with a new idea. One of our members, an architect, had just recovered from a serious illness and needed some cheering up. He was asked to design the next float for the Rotary Club.

The result was "Santa's Workshop." It had an oversized workbench with Santa's helpers (elves) played by the Rotarians. The workbench came up to our shoulders and the tools were huge. Since every item on the float was oversized, it made the men seem smaller. In order to emphasize the scale even more, a large wooden wall was erected at the front of the trailer, blocking the view of the tractor. This wooden wall represented the wall of the workshop and it was huge.

As the float moved down Main Street, people noticed how high this wall was and began shouting, "You will never get under the railroad bridge." Soon a crowd was tagging along to see our pending disaster at the bridge.

The truck stopped short of the bridge. The elves got off the float, looked at the problem, and scratched their heads. The crowd roared with laughter, and a few "I told you so!" shouts were heard. The elves jumped back on the float, loosened several ropes, and the wall was lowered down. The crowd clapped. Once under the railroad bridge the wall was raised again.

In the cab of the truck, the architect smiled and laughed. Sometimes work is the best therapy to get you well.

The Hungarian Lady

In the late 1970's we hired a lady named Helen, a widow, to

clean our offices. Her sister-in-law applied for the job for her, as Helen spoke no English. At that time we had another employee who spoke Hungarian so we figured we could manage.

Helen had an eleven-year-old son and they had just arrived from Hungary, which in the late 1970's was still a communist satellite state of the Soviet Union. Amazingly he spoke English. They lived with her brother and sister-in-law. One morning Helen arrived at work in tears, carrying a suitcase, with her son in tow. The sister-in-law had kicked them out of the house.

Helen had no place to live. My mother lived next door to my office and she had spare bedrooms in her house. So out of the goodness of her heart, she decided to take in Helen and her son. Everything started to work out well. Helen cooked, mom helped the son with his schoolwork, and Helen began to learn English.

One night my mother called me at two o'clock in the morning saying that Helen was sick. When I got to the house I realized that Helen was very sick. I called the police and asked them to get the first aid squad. Soon there was a knock at the door. I let the policeman in. He saw that the patient was upstairs in the house so he called for backup.

At that time I noticed that the son was missing. I searched and found him hiding under the bed. He told me that he was afraid of the police. I explained that they were here to help us. The first aid squad soon arrived. The boy watched his mother get loaded onto a stretcher and carried down the stairs to the ambulance. My mom rode with Helen to the hospital.

The boy was left with me and he was very nervous as he asked who would pay for all of this. I explained that the police were paid by the town of Metuchen and that the men from the first aid squad were volunteers and their service was free.

He was amazed that two men would get up at two o'clock in the morning to take a stranger to the hospital and that the police were there to help.

WELCOME TO AMERICA!

The Traffic Stop

Years ago a very proper lady friend of mine was pulled over in her car by a police officer. She rolled down her window as he approached.

"Where are you coming from?" he asked. She replied, "I am coming from Barry's Butcher Shop. I just bought a beautiful pot roast. My husband loves pot roast with the special gravy I make." She then proceeded to tell him how she made the gravy.

"Where are you going?" asked the officer as he took out his ticket book.

"I am going to Schultz's Butcher Shop in the next town. I am going to buy some of his best large pork chops and some of his sausage. I will have him cut pockets in the pork chops so I can stuff sausage inside them."

"Do you know that you were doing thirty-seven miles per hour in a twenty-five mile per hour zone?" he questioned, as he pulled out his ballpoint pen.

"Oh officer, I didn't know that. Thank you so much for telling me," she responded as she rolled up the window and drove away.

I have told this story to many police officers and I asked what they would have done in this case. The universal reply has been "Let her go!"

And that is what the police officer did.

Greece

In 1979, my son Martin "Skip" Jessen, a civil engineer, was working in Greece for an American construction company that was building an aircraft maintenance facility for the Hellenic (Greek) Air Force and Olympic Airlines. My wife and I decided to go for a visit. As we boarded the plane I asked the stewardess, "What is the movie?"

She answered, "Grease."

"Oh great, a travelogue, and we are going to visit Greece."

"It is not a travelogue. It is a movie with John Travolta."

"Will I like it?" I asked.

She answered, "I don't know anything about you."

I told her, "My favorite actor is John Wayne and my favorite composer is John Philip Sousa."

"You won't like it," she said, and she was right.

While touring in Greece my son Skip was driving to the town of Delphi to see the home of the Delphi oracle. We got lost. We were on a dirt road, on a flat treeless plain, with no people or buildings around. As we approached a cross-road, another car approached from the left. We flagged them down and

Skip, speaking his best Greek, asked them for directions. They shook their heads and replied in German. Then Skip asked them in French. They answered in Italian.

Finally we tried English, and it turned out they were from Cleveland, Ohio!

My Mother Was a Teacher

My mother, Hannah Hughes Jessen, graduated from a two-year normal school, West Chester Normal School (West Chester University of Pennsylvania today), and became a school teacher. Normal schools were created to train high school graduates to be teachers. Her first job was in Perth Amboy, New Jersey, in the 1920's. When I was six, she began teaching in the Metuchen Public Schools. Then the hard times began. The Great Depression really hit home. She lost her job to someone better connected. She could get only part-time substitute work.

In those days children who had survived polio (infantile paralysis) were crippled to the extent that they could not attend school. My mother became a bedside teacher in Metuchen and Raritan Township. Each student got instruction one hour a day, five days a week. She would take buses and walk to their houses. She walked miles every day in all types of weather.

When World War II started, the economy got better. She was hired to teach seventh and eighth grade mathematics at Metuchen's Franklin School. She loved it. I remember her marking papers at the kitchen table with a big red pencil. Many times she worked out the problem so the student would learn how it was done.

She didn't believe in homework, "You give me your full attention every day in class and you won't need homework," was her refrain.

The classes were large; sometimes thirty-five to forty students, but discipline was not a problem. She would raise her hand holding a yardstick if anyone got out of line. She used to walk up to the person disrupting her class and say, "One, two, three, four, five, if I get to ten you'd better duck!" One year the kids gave her a mink-handled yardstick for Christmas.

In later years she went to Rutgers University part-time to get a teaching degree. Even though she had been teaching for many years, the new requirement was for all teachers to have four-year degrees, so she had to return to college. She thought most of the teaching courses were a waste of time that could be better spent studying the subject to be taught. She graduated in the same class of 1950 that I did. I bet that hasn't happened very often—that a mother and son both received their college diplomas on the same day at the same college.

She retired at sixty-five but kept substituting until she was eighty. One time she was asked to substitute in a Spanish class. She did not know any Spanish, but the school administration said she was their last resort as all the other substitutes turned it down.

The students figured they would get a free ride to goof off. Mom announced to each class, "We are not going to waste a week. Schools don't teach square root anymore, so this week you will all learn how to do square root." And they did.

Mom had the gift of teaching. She loved the kids and the

kids loved her. She always had a special place in her heart for the kids who needed a little more love.

Advice on Getting Married

Old folks are always giving advice to young people. When I was young I got lots of advice, most of which I ignored, to my regret. But some I listened to. On looking for a wife, my dad's advice was, "Find someone who will put up with you." I did.

After I got married, he advised me, "Remember you cannot win, and, if you think you are winning, you are in big trouble."

My advice to young men getting married is: "Buy your bride a nice gift. Wrap it in plain paper. Then hide it someplace. Someday you will need it."

I also tell the bride of this advice, and then I add: "If you find the gift, leave it alone and when someday he finally brings it to you, be gracious."

Usually I also explain that birthdays and anniversaries are important to women, while to men the date of the next Super Bowl is of prime importance.

God certainly made men and women different.

Weddings and Wedding Receptions

Over the years I have been to a lot of weddings, so I know what to expect. However, there was one that was different. The minister, in the middle of the ceremony, had the couple face each other. He said, "I want you to look at each other carefully. I am telling you that what you see is what you get. If you have any idea of changing that person or improving that person, then let's stop right now."

The couple nodded to each other and then hugged. It took a tremendous amount of willpower for me not to jump up and say Amen!

The wedding receptions usually start out with cocktails and friends and relatives talking. Many have a lot to say, catching up on old times, discussing aches, pains, cures, and just general enjoyment of each other's company. We sit down to eat at carefully selected table assignments and have more conversation.

Then the music starts. You know it is loud when you watch the water in the water glasses vibrate. We are now shouting into another person's ear and it becomes only a two person conversation because everyone else can't hear what we are saying. Did we come here to hear the music or talk to friends and relatives? Wouldn't it be better to have soft background music until after the bouquet toss and garter incident? Then the music could be cranked up, the people with normal hearing could go home, and those that enjoy the vibration could have their fill.

One wedding reception was different. When my son Skip

and daughter-in-law Linda married, I volunteered to pay for the band. During the reception I met the bandleader and I handed him the check representing his payment. I then said, "This second check represents your tip. Notice that it is blank. The louder you play, the smaller your tip will be, while the softer you play, the larger your tip will be." The music was wonderful!

Husband Improvement

A teamster friend of mine is sometimes known as a rough tough union leader. Once when he was attending his son's Little League game, his wife gave him the warning to "Behave yourself." At the game, the umpire failed to show up—no umpire meant no game. An appeal was made to the audience for someone to volunteer their services. No response.

Then the head of the league approached my friend and persuaded him to umpire the game for the good of the teams and their loyal fans.

The game started and many of the fans disputed the umpire calls. The language got rougher. One couple was extremely loud and had a stunning gutter vocabulary.

My friend finally snapped, stopped the game, walked over to the bleachers, grabbed the offensive fan by his coat, hoisted him into the air, and growled, "I have never umpired a baseball game before. I am doing the best I can. If you can do better, the job is yours."

From his lofty position above the crowd with his feet dangling in the air, the fan meekly replied, "You are doing just fine."

My friend gave him a good shaking and said, "Then shut up!" The game continued and can probably be described as the best behaved Little League game in history; with only positive comments from any of the fans.

On the way home from the game, his wife, a husband improver, listed his misdeeds. How could she ever face her friends again? Their son would be thrown out of the league, and so on. When they arrived home, the telephone was ringing. The wife answered, and covering the mouthpiece said, "It's the league president. Now you are going to get it."

My friend took the phone, listened, and said, "No thank you," and hung up. "What was that all about?" asked the wife.

"He wanted me to be a permanent umpire."

The Ladder Story

There are several fruit trees in our backyard. In the early spring I would prune them by climbing up the trees. When I reached sixty-five years of age my wife gave me a twelve-foot ladder and an ultimatum—no more climbing trees.

So one fine spring day I had my pruning shears, a set of loppers, and a saw—all hanging from my belt. I was on the ladder's top step where it says, "DO NOT STAND HERE," and I was reaching out to get the last sucker clipped off.

Suddenly the ladder shot out from under me and I was hanging from the limb. Then I felt a cool breeze blowing where it shouldn't have been. With all the extra weight on my belt, my pants had slipped down and stopped at my ankles. I was in a bad way. After a lot of kicking and squirming, finally my pants dropped off.

The trip down the tree was very painful—bare legs and sharp prickly bark.

When I got down I saw my neighbor lady watching and laughing. She called out, "I didn't know whether to call the police or America's Funniest Home Videos."

Getting Cultured

My wife Barbara arranged three "culture" trips for us to the State Theatre in New Brunswick, New Jersey, to see: (1) *The Nutcracker,* (2) *Salute to Vienna,* and (3) the Irish Guards with the Royal Regiment of Scotland. The first was a ballet, the second was a symphony orchestra (mostly strings), and the third was a brass band along with bagpipes and drums.

Don't tell my wife this, but I really liked the last one the best. These British musicians were dressed in their scarlet tunic uniforms with tall bearskin caps. They started off playing "Hands Across the Sea" by John Philip Sousa. Then the audience stood for the English national anthem "God save the Queen." In America we use the same tune with different words and call it "My Country, 'Tis of Thee." Then they played the

"Star Spangled Banner." The audience broke into song and sang lustfully. I got all choked up. After a long applause, the bagpipes and drums took over. The audience was ecstatic as they cheered and clapped.

Something unexpected happened next. A red coat musician with a violin came on stage and began skillfully playing with the band. The sound of the violin was clearly heard with the loud playing of the band. My grandson, Robert "Bobby" Jessen, who gave up his computer for a whole evening just to please me, explained, "He is amped up." Translation: A small radio transmitter in the violin sends the sound to a powerful amplification system.

As a tribute to the American Armed Forces they played the appropriate service songs. Each veteran stood up as their song was played. I stood up for "Anchors Aweigh," which they played twice, making me very happy. As I looked around the audience I realized the next generation of Americans were enthusiastic, very polite, good singers of the national anthem, and maybe there is hope for America after all. In my opinion the biggest threat to America's future is the United States Congress.

One final thought: The national anthem was written by Francis Scott Key during the War of 1812, as he watched the British fleet bombard Fort McHenry at Baltimore, Maryland. "The rocket's red glare, the bombs bursting in air," was all aimed at the Americans inside the fort. Times change and the British are no longer our enemy, but our friends, who send their bands to entertain us. As my favorite Englishman Sir Winston Churchill once said, "It is good that two nations can join together when only separated by a common language."

Pocketknives

I got my first pocketknife when I was in third grade. It was a Boy Scout knife with a big blade, a small blade, a screwdriver, a bottle opener, and a can opener. My father, Martin Jessen, always made sure that both blades were really sharp.

In fifth grade I had to share my pocketknife with other boys. In class the teacher would inspect our fingernails and if they were too dirty, a friend would ask to borrow my pocketknife to clean his nails. The small knife blade was perfect for this task. In case you are wondering, yes we did carry pocketknives to school and we did not get in trouble for doing so. Times have changed.

Today I carry a Swiss Army pocketknife. It is a lot like the Boy Scout pocketknife.

One of my problems that I must constantly guard against is keeping my pocketknife away from the government. They like my pocketknife so much that they are always trying to take it away from me.

Recently we visited Washington, D.C., where every government building had a metal detector. I found out that the government would confiscate pocketknives and would not give them back. Looking back, I should have left my pocketknife at home, but I didn't.

Every time we entered a government building I would hide my pocketknife in a flower bed. It was pansy time, so I picked the yellow pansy closest to the entrance and buried my pocketknife one hand span away. After the tour, I would dig up my pocketknife. You would not believe some of the strange looks that people would give me. One young boy watched me dig up my pocketknife. He was totally amazed! As I left, I saw the boy furiously digging in the same flower bed.

My system was working very well until I got to a government building that did not have a flower bed near the entrance. Fortunately, in front of the building was a big statue of Benjamin Franklin—sitting down.

I climbed up onto the statue and left my pocketknife in his lap. Later, when I retrieved my pocketknife, I almost thought I saw Ben give me a smile!

Bibliography

Bluejackets' Manual. Naval Institute Press, Annapolis, Maryland, 1943.

Clark, C. B., *C. B. Clark's Johnstown Directory and Citizens' Register.* Altoona, Pennsylvania, 1889. Available from: www.camgenpa.com/books/1889Dir/. Accessed 30 June 2011.

Dictionary of American Naval Fighting Ships, Volume I (1959), reprinted with corrections 1964; Volume II (1963), reprinted with corrections 1969, reprint 1977; Volume III (1968); Volume IV (1969); Volume V (1970); Volume VI (1976); Volume VII (1981); Volume VIII (1981). Navy Department, Office of the Chief of Naval Operations, Naval History Division, Washington, United States Government Printing Office, Washington, D.C.

Jessen, Martin D. World War II letters, 14 November 1944 – 24 May 1946. Unpublished.

Jessen, Martin D. Korean War letters, 27 April 1951 – 4 April 1952. Unpublished.

Jessen, Martin D. Korean War diary, 2 May 1951 – 12 April 1952. Unpublished.

Log Book of the U.S.S. *Albert T. Harris* (DE-447), 3 June 1945 – 6 June 1946. National Archives and Records Administration, College Park, Maryland.

Log Book of the U.S.S. *Conserver* (ARS-39), 1 May 1951 – 29

February 1952. National Archives and Records Administration, College Park, Maryland.

Log Book of the U.S.S. *Current* (ARS-22), 1 February 1952 – 30 April 1952. National Archives and Records Administration, College Park, Maryland.

Log Book of the U.S.S. *General M. B. Stewart* (AP-140), 22 April 1945 – 25 May 1945. National Archives and Records Administration, College Park, Maryland.

Log Book of the U.S.S. LST 1015, 1 November 1945 – 30 November 1945. National Archives and Records Administration, College Park, Maryland.

Manchester, William. *American Caesar: Douglas MacArthur 1880–1964*. Little, Brown and Company, Boston, 1978.

McCullough, David. *The Johnstown Flood*. Simon & Schuster, New York, 1968.

Origins of Navy Terminology. Available from: www.navy.mil/navydata/traditions/html/navyterm.html. Accessed 8 April 2011.

Sailing Report of Changes U.S.S. *Albert T. Harris* (DE-447) for the twenty-first day of June 1945, pages 17–18. National Archives and Records Administration, College Park, Maryland.

War Diary of the U.S.S. *Albert T. Harris* (DE-447) for the period 1–30 June 1945. National Archives and Records Administration, College Park, Maryland.

Glossary of Naval Terms

Bow: Forward (fore) end of the hull of a ship.

Bridge: The raised platform in the forward part of a ship where navigation and steering take place.

Bulkhead: A wall or partition within a ship. Decks and bulkheads divide a ship into numerous water-tight compartments.

Conn: Control of the ship's movements. The officer who has the responsibility for the navigation and safety of the ship has the conn.

Convoy: A group of noncombatant ships such as troop transports, fuel ships, cargo ships, etc., proceeding under the escort of one or more warships detailed for their protection.

Davit: A deck structure usually made of steel that is used to cradle a boat for storage and to hoist a boat over the side of the ship for launching.

Depth charges: Anti-submarine weapon consisting of cylindrical cans filled with TNT and fitted with an explosion mechanism that is set to detonate at a specific depth.

Deck: The horizontal structure on a ship that forms the "roof" for the hull of the ship, or one of the different levels in a ship. Also the term for the floor of a ship.

Fantail: Extreme rear of the ship.

Galley: Kitchen.

Head: Toilet and washroom.

Hedgehog: Anti-submarine weapon consisting of small spigot mortar bombs that exploded on contact.

Officer of the deck: Officer in charge of the ship during a watch, one of the periods (usually four hours) into which the day is divided.

Port: The port side of a ship is on the left-hand side looking forward toward the bow.

Quartermaster: Enlisted crewman responsible for the ship's navigation, steering, and maintenance of nautical charts.

Radar: Radio direction and ranging. An instrument for determining the presence of objects by using echoes from radio waves.

Rudder: The vertical underwater blade used to steer a ship.

SA Radar: Air radar, bedspring shaped, used for detecting aircraft. Also used for navigational purposes, SA radar's longer range would detect land further away than would the SU radar.

SCAJAP: Shipping Control Authority for the Japanese Merchant Marine. SCAJAP was originally established after World War II for the repatriation of Japanese war personnel. During the Korean War SCAJAP crews of Japanese Imperial Navy veterans of World War II operated LSTs (Landing Ship Tanks).

Sonar: *Sound navigation and ranging.* Attached to the keel of a ship, this instrument emits underwater pulses of sound that radiate out from the ship, parallel to the surface of the sea. By listening for echoes, it was used to detect underwater objects, specifically submarines.

Starboard: The starboard side of a ship is on the right-hand side looking forward toward the bow.

Stern: Rear or after (aft) end of a ship.

SU Radar: Surface radar for locating ships, surfaced submarines, land, buoys, and other objects on the surface of the sea.

About the Author

Martin Daniel Jessen was born in Perth Amboy, New Jersey, in 1926 and grew up in Metuchen, New Jersey. He entered active service in the United States Naval Reserve on 23 June 1944, at the age of seventeen. He served in the Pacific as quartermaster aboard the destroyer escort USS *Albert T. Harris* (DE-447) from 18 June 1945 to 5 June 1946. In 1950 he received a Bachelor of Science degree in civil engineering from Rutgers University.

With the outbreak of the Korean War, Ensign Jessen was called up by the Navy as a reservist on 2 January 1951. In April 1951, he graduated from the United States Naval Salvage & Diving School at Bayonne, New Jersey, as a qualified diver to one hundred fifty feet and as a salvage officer.

Following salvage school, Lieutenant (junior grade) Jessen was the diving and salvage officer, morale officer, medical officer, gunnery officer, and navigator aboard the rescue salvage ship the USS *Conserver* (ARS-39). In February 1952, he was transferred to the rescue salvage ship the USS *Current* (ARS-22) serving as first lieutenant and diving and salvage officer in the Pacific during the Korean War.

In civilian life, for over thirty years Marty owned and operated an excavating business, Arnolt Bros. Inc.; *The Diligent Diggers of Dignified Dirt*. He still works today as president of Victorian Office Rentals, Inc.

Marty has been a Delaware and Raritan Canal Commissioner for over thirty-five years. He has been active in numerous government, charitable, and civic organizations. Marty and his beloved wife Barbara have been married for over sixty years and reside in Metuchen, New Jersey.

Marty and his daughter, Nancy Jessen, are currently working on his memoir, *A Clean Place to Eat and Sleep*.

Front Cover Photograph: Navigator, Lieutenant (junior grade) Martin D. Jessen, United States Naval Reserve, using sextant to take noon sun site. Standing in twenty-millimeter gun tub aboard the rescue salvage ship USS *Conserver* (ARS-39), Western Pacific, 1951. (Author's Collection)

Back Cover Photograph: Diver, Lieutenant (junior grade) Martin D. Jessen, United States Naval Reserve, in diving suit standing on the stage with diver's tender holding the stage, and the air, telephone, and life lines. Aboard the barge *Mary Ann*, Kwajalein Atoll, Marshall Islands, 17 July 1951. (Author's Collection)